FIELD HOCKEY

An International Team Sport

PRENTICE-HALL INTERNATIONAL, INC., *London*
PRENTICE-HALL OF AUSTRALIA, PTY., LTD., *Sydney*
PRENTICE-HALL FRANCE, S.A.R.L., *Paris*
PRENTICE-HALL OF JAPAN, INC., *Tokyo*
PRENTICE-HALL DE MEXICO, S.A., *Mexico City*
PRENTICE-HALL OF CANADA, LTD., *Toronto*

Helen T. Mackey

FIELD HOCKEY
An International Team Sport

PRENTICE-HALL, INC.
Englewood Cliffs, N.J.

© 1963 by
Prentice-Hall, Inc.
Englewood Cliffs, N.J.

*Library of Congress
Catalog Card No. 63-11098*

Printed in the United States of America
C- 3 1 4 4 5

Current printing (last digit):

13   12   11   10   9   8   7   6   5

DEDICATION

This book is dedicated
to all the hockey enthusiasts
past, present, and future
who have or will have shared with me the
wonderful joys and breadth and depth of
experience and friendship to be found in
the world-wide game of Field Hockey.

H.T.M.

Since the time of the ancient Greeks, we have always felt that there was a close relationship between a strong, vital mind and physical fitness. I don't think we have to read the results of tests which we have seen during the last ten years to realize that because of the generosity of nature, and the way our society has developed, there has been less emphasis here on national vigor, national vitality and physical well-being than in many other countries of the world.

We do not want in the United States a nation of spectators. We want a nation of participants in the vigorous life. It is my hope that mothers and fathers across the United States will be concerned about this phase of their children's development; that the communities will be concerned, will make it possible for boys and girls to participate fully in physical activities; and that men and women who have reached the age of maturity will continue their own participation in this phase of the national vigor—national life.

We must make sure that as our life becomes more sophisticated, more urbanized, we don't lose this priceless facet of our national character—the physical vitality which is closely allied to intellectual vigor and spiritual strength.

President John F. Kennedy

Hockey for women is one of the few truly amateur sports and therefore will always have an ardent . . . following of true sportswomen. While National and International matches have been held each season since 1894, there have never been any championship matches held, as the game calls for united initiative and creative ability on the part of each player on the team. The merely mechanical, technical player will never become an advanced hockey player. This fact is clearly illustrated at all international gatherings. Perhaps in this distinctive quality of first class hockey lies its . . . fascination for its players.

Constance M. K. Applebee

PREFACE

This book is prepared for anyone interested in hockey—students, players, coaches, and umpires. Photographs are used throughout the book to depict individual skills, techniques, and tactics, as well as team play, team tactics, and game strategy. The author describes the use and performance of each stroke, tackle, and dodge and gives pointers for each; lists helpful hints concerning what a good player does or does not do in connection with each play and suggestions for correction of weaknesses; and suggests practices (skills, drills, or games) to aid the player or coach in achieving expert stickwork and a highly developed game.

A special feature of the book is the consistent lineup of the team players with relation to many game situations illustrated, so that each of the eleven players may readily locate the directions for her play.

The eleven positions on the team are discussed for attack (offense) and defense play. Descriptions are clearly illustrated by means of pictures and charts.

The author's experience as player, coach, selector, and umpire has provided for inclusion of material known to be necessary to each of these groups for development of an excellent game. Action photographs bring life to the word description and bring the living game to the view of the reader.

The author extends appreciation to her many colleagues and friends who have helped to make this book possible.

Special thanks are expressed to Miss Dorothy Sullivan, Milton

Academy, for helpful assistance and suggestions; Mr. Roger Hardy, State College at Salem, Massachusetts, Mr. Earl J. Cunningham, Milton, Massachusetts, and Mr. Harris W. Reynolds, Brookline, Massachusetts for photograph work; to my sister, Dr. Ann Mackey, State College at Framingham, Framingham, Massachusetts, for her assistance in posing for several of the photographs; to Miss Maude V. Sharp, Lake Pine, Marlton, New Jersey, Miss Gertrude Hooper, Milton, Massachusetts, and Mrs. Joyce Cran Barry, Marblehead, Massachusetts, for critical reviews of the manuscript.

TABLE OF CONTENTS

FIELD HOCKEY

An International Team Sport

1

The potential field hockey player or coach, in order to get "under way," needs an intelligent overview of the game in its following aspects: background information as to how the game developed; equipment used; the hockey field; officials, and lineup of players and a general description of play, including the duration of the game.

Development of Women's Field Hockey

Field Hockey is of recent origin in the United States. Miss Constance M. K. Applebee, a member of the British College of Physical Education, figured prominently in the development of the game among Americans.

During the summer of 1901 Miss Applebee introduced the game at the Harvard College Summer School of Physical Education, demon-

Getting Under Way

strating the game to leaders and students. She used shinny or ice hockey sticks, an indoor baseball, and chalk lines drawn on the concrete yard at the back of the Harvard gymnasium. That fall, instruction in the game was arranged for students at Vassar College, Wellesley, Mount Holyoke, Smith, Radcliffe and Bryn Mawr. Miss Applebee took twenty-four hockey sticks and a cricket ball to all the colleges. The sticks had been discarded by an Englishman who had been unsuccessful in developing the interest of American men and women in Field Hockey.

In the spring of 1902 hockey was begun by many schools, including the Boston Normal School of Gymnastics, which gave a hockey training course for students and graduates in order that they might introduce the game into both public and private schools and colleges.

The Philadelphia Hockey Association, comprising four clubs, was formed in 1904. Shortly afterward, organized teams appeared in Boston and New York. In 1920, a group of players made a tour of England, and as a result of this tour a representative English team visited this country in the fall of 1921. The team played games and gave instructional help in several schools and colleges in Philadelphia, New York, Boston, and Baltimore. Three of the English Touring Team players remained in this country for several weeks, lecturing and coaching at colleges as far west as the University of Chicago and the University of Wisconsin.

In January, 1922, the two existing associations in Philadelphia and Boston formed the United States Field Hockey Association (U.S.F.H.A.), which is the governing body of women's field hockey. The objective of the organization was to spread and advance the interests of hockey throughout the United States. It made plans to achieve uniformity in the rules and equipment, and to unite players in clubs and sections for the purpose of bringing together participants from all over the country. In November, 1922, the U.S.F.H.A. sponsored its first tournament, with participation by four local associations. The first officers of the U.S.F.H.A. were: President, Mrs. Edward B. Krumbhaar, Philadelphia Cricket Club; Vice Presidents, Miss Cynthia Wesson, University of Wisconsin, and Miss Fannie Crenshaw, Westhampton College, Virginia; Secretary, Miss Helen Ferguson, Germantown Cricket Club, Philadelphia; and Treasurer, Mrs. Charles Loring of the Boston Association.

In the fall of 1922 and for the next four years, the U.S.F.H.A., through the All-England Women's Hockey Association, arranged to have a group of English players come to this country to teach and coach hockey in schools, normal schools, and clubs in order to improve and develop the game in the United States. In September, 1922, Miss Applebee started a fall camp which is still carried on in the "Poconos," Pennsylvania. The "hockey camp" idea provides intensified training and inspiration under the leadership of top-notch coaches who give expert instruction in the improvement of knowledge, skill, and play. Hockey camps have now spread to all parts of the country.

The United States Field Hockey Association is comprised of nine sectional organizations: Great Lakes, Mideast, Midwest, New-Atlantic, Northeast, Pacific Northwest, Pacific Southwest, Philadelphia, and Southeast. Each section, headed by a chairman, is made up of innumerable local associations.

To qualify as a local association, the group must have at least three active clubs which must play a minimum of four games each season. In order to play on an association team, a player must be at least seventeen years of age and must have been a citizen or resident of the United States for two years. A biannual publication called the Field Hockey – Lacrosse Guide, which may be ordered from The Division for Girls and Women's Sports, 1201 Sixteenth St., N.W., Washington 6, D.C., lists personnel of local associations through whom information may be obtained as to how any player may join a club.

Each year, in the local association, a Selection Committee names the "First" and "Reserve" teams to play at a tournament conducted by the section. At the sectional tournament, another Selection Committee names the section's First and Reserve teams to compete at the National Tournament, which is arranged by a National Tournament Committee. The tournament is usually held at Thanksgiving, in a section of the country previously decided upon by the U.S.F.H.A. Executive Committee. The local association of the selected area serves

Fig. 1. The National Field Hockey Tournament, 1962. Miss Constance Applebee and Helen Mackey, U.S.F.H.A. Umpiring Chairman.

Fig. 2. The parade of the Sectional Teams at the U.S.F.H.A. National Tournament at Sidwell Friend's School, Washington, D.C., 1959.

as hostess. At the National Tournament, a Selection Committee of the U.S.F.H.A. names the United States First Team and the United States Reserve Team whose members are the outstanding players of this country. In 1959, the Vice President of the United States officially opened the National Tournament Games, held that year at the Sidwell Friend's School, Washington, D.C.

In January, 1924, the United States Team began its first official tour during which they played in the British Isles and Paris, France. At the conclusion of the tour, in March, the players and representatives of several countries participated in a hockey conference near London.

As a result of the hockey conference, the International Federation of Women's Hockey Associations (I.F.W.H.A.) was formed in 1927 by the United States and eight other countries. The I.F.W.H.A. is now comprised of 25 nations: Argentina, Australia, Austria, Belgium, British Guiana, Canada, Ceylon, Denmark, England, France, Germany, India, Ireland, Jamaica, Kenya, Pan Malaya, Netherlands, New Zealand, Scotland, South Africa, Spain, Switzerland, Trinidad, United States, and Wales. The aims that were set forth by the I.F.W.H.A. were to standardize and popularize the game of field hockey among women of all nations, with conferences scheduled every three years in different parts of the world. Triennial conferences and tours were held in Switzerland in 1930, Denmark in 1933, U.S.A. in 1936, South Africa in 1950, England in 1953, Australia in 1956, and Holland in 1959. Present plans are for the Federation to meet on a four-year basis, the first of which events will take place in the United States in the fall of 1963. The U.S.F.H.A. will be hostess to the world organization for field hockey, officially titled the Eighth Quadrennial Conference and Tour of the International Federation of Women's Hockey Associations. A two-weeks' conference for games and discussion of international rules and hockey problems will be combined with extended tours offered to the international players. Thus, field hockey, by fostering international education, skill, and friendship becomes an important vehicle for implementation of one of the nation's first goals: world peace through real understanding and friendship among each country's citizens.

Recognizing the fact that good umpiring promotes good play, the U.S.F.H.A. formed an Umpiring Committee in 1924. This committee publishes an Operating Code which clarifies the committee organization and duties, and indicates the requirements for national, sectional, and local ratings, found on an early page of the Field Hockey – Lacrosse Guide. The duties of the committee are to interpret the official rules, to give ratings after written examinations and practical trials, and to advise clubs and schools on rules and umpiring problems. The U.S.F.H.A. awards a "National Umpire" rating to those umpires who have demonstrated outstanding ability.

The Division for Girls and Women's Sports (D.G.W.S.), of the American Association for Health, Physical Education, and Recreation of the National Education Association, is the governing body for standards and playing rules for girls' sports. The D.G.W.S. adopted the official rules for field hockey, and, with a Committee appointed by the U.S.F.H.A., works on field hockey policies and procedures. The

FIG. 3. Miss Constance Applebee and the Scottish Touring Team at Wellesley College, Wellesley, Mass., 1951.

Field Hockey – Lacrosse Guide (mentioned above), published by the D.G.W.S., contains the official rules, articles of interest, and listings of national, sectional, and local committees and officers. "The Eagle," a U.S.F.H.A. publication containing technical and coaching articles, keeps hockey enthusiasts informed of special events.

Several committees of the U.S.F.H.A. are active in promoting the work of the organization. In addition to the National Tournament Committees, Selection Committees, and Umpiring Committees previously mentioned, there are special committees on Extension, Equipment, Insurance, Publicity, and Technical Service. There are also numerous committees which work on such additional activities as constitutional questions, membership and honorary membership recommendations, nominations for officers, and local sectional problems.

Equipment

Quality equipment is the most economical. It is always advisable to buy from a reputable firm, for to buy the cheapest equipment, or equipment advertised as a "bargain," is often false economy and necessitates frequent replacement. Therefore, the matter of equipment, even for beginners, should be considered seriously and the selections made carefully.

Stick:

In choosing a stick, the main features to consider are length and weight. A stick that is too long is difficult to use and is awkward to handle; a stick that is too short will handicap play as it will shorten the reach, cause topping of the ball, or require stooping to stop the ball. Such difficulties with the stick will slow the play.

To test for proper length of stick, the player stands in an upright position, grasps the top of the handle of the stick with both hands, and swings it backward and forward. If the blade of the stick scarcely touches the ground, the stick is the proper length.

A stick should not be heavier than can be handled comfortably by a player. To get the "feel" of the stick, several should be tried as if the player were standing ready to drive. After handling and swinging the different sticks, choice can be made of one that feels comfortable.

There are no "left-handed" sticks in field hockey.

The following list may be used as a general guide in the selection of a stick:

Height of Player	*Length of Stick*	*Weight of Stick*
5 ft. 8 inches	37 inches	20 or 19 ounces
5 ft. 6 inches	36 inches	20 ounces
5 ft. 4 inches	35 inches	19 ounces
5 ft. 2 inches	34 inches	18 or 17 ounces
5 ft.	33 inches	17 ounces
4 ft. 10 inches	32 inches	17 ounces
4 ft. 8 inches	31 inches	17 ounces
4 ft. 6 inches	30 inches	17 ounces

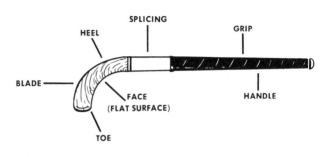

FIG. 4. Field hockey stick and its parts. A stick with the head or blade made of ash and with the grain of the wood following the curve of the blade should be selected; other types of blades will break and splinter.

There are different types of sticks, such as the Indian Head style and English type. (See Figure 5.) However, the toe of all sticks should be rounded. There are sticks made for juniors who begin to learn the elements of the game as early as grade four. A lightweight stick is recommended for their use.

After determination of length and weight, flexibility and resiliency should be considered. To ensure resistance and strength, the handle of the stick should be made of cane, recognizable by the myriads of little holes visible at the top of the handle.

In the handle, through this cane, should be at least two parallel or cross-rubber insertions. These spliced insertions will prevent stinging of the hands when the ball is hit, give more drive to the ball, and insure better ball control.

Care of the Stick: The better the care given to a stick, the longer it will last. Immediately after use in the rain, or on wet ground, it should be wiped and left to dry. Any stick which begins to fray at the edges should be sandpapered, when dry, and waxed. If the stick splinters it should be shaved down, and the shaving process worked toward the open end of the splinter; it must then be sanded and protected by a piece of adhesive tape. Only one layer of tape should be used, as heavy taping will unbalance the stick. If the rubber grip rots and dries, it can be replaced at a nominal fee. However, a grip applicator may be purchased or made by the player who prefers to care for her own stick.

During the season, the blade of the stick should be wiped occasionally with an oily (linseed oil) cloth. At the end of the season it should be cleaned with steel wool, rubbed with beeswax, wrapped in an oily cloth, and stored, lying flat to prevent warping, in a cool, dry place.

Balls:

An "official" hockey ball must be used in games. In common use are those with a stitched or seamed leather cover coated with white enamel paint, which helps to preserve the ball under wet conditions, and the Chingford ball, made of plastic. The latter is not only less expensive than the leather type, but does not need constant painting, does not lose its shape, and lasts longer. When it is necessary to clean the plastic ball, any cleaner may be used with a brush. Another official ball is the Tugite, made of chrome leather. The future will undoubtedly bring the use of balls made with other materials.

Practice balls are inexpensive composition balls which can be wiped off with a wet cloth.

Shinguards:

It is strongly urged that players wear short, light shinguards to protect their legs from stick and ball injuries. Shinguards do not affect a player's speed or dexterity, but give a great deal of protection to the ankle bones as well as the shins, thus giving the players confidence.

Shinguards are lightweight although made of a sturdy canvas material, well-padded, with leather straps. The straps should be fastened so that the buckles are on the outsides of the legs. Also available are lightweight, strapless shinguards which are worn under the socks or stockings. Shinguards should be stored in a box in a dry place.

Shoes and Socks:

Many players wear hockey shoes made of black canvas with rubber studs or bars. These can be purchased at most sporting goods stores. Some players prefer leather shoes with leather cleats which do give better footing on muddy grounds, but these are heavier and stiffer than the canvas hockey sneakers. Heavy shoes are unnecessary and interfere with swift action. The foot gear should be light, flexible, well-fitting, and cleated. A cleated shoe or sneaker enables a player to stop and start more quickly and to have better control. Players are not allowed to wear shoes with metal cleats.

FIG. 5. The English type stick and the Indian Head style with a shorter head. Player No. 4 holds the Indian Head style stick. The second girl from the left holds a stick with a plastic-coated blade for added durability. The goalkeeper's pads come in varying sizes. The taller goalkeeper is wearing kicking boots whereas the shorter goalkeeper is wearing kickers. Both girls on the right are wearing shinguards.

FIG. 6. These girls show the different styles of cleats on the bottom of their shoes or sneakers.

Woolen socks keep the feet warm, absorb perspiration, and act as a cushion in the shoe. As for stockings or long tights, many players like them for extra warmth as well as for better looks, but this is an individual choice.

Uniform:

Tunics, shorts and blouses, or short pleated skirts and blouses are considered desirable for playing field hockey, because they allow for freedom of movement. Pleated tunics of a bold color are used by many teams because they look neat, are comfortable to wear, and easily distinguished. They fit loosely and do not have to be altered when used by various individuals; this proves economical for schools and teams. Shorts and pleated skirts must be fitted to the individual in order to look well.

Pinnies:

Pinnies—straight pieces of cloth worn over the shoulders, reaching below the waist, and held around the waistline with sashes—should be available for use when needed to aid in differentiating teams on the field. Pinnies should be of a bold, distinguishable color that is not used by any other team in the area, and they should be made of durable material. Pinnies may be labeled for beginners by using letters, designating positions, that are sewn on or put on with chalk, adhesive tape, or iron-on tape.

Goalkeeper Equipment

Stick:

The same general rules for choosing a stick apply to the goalkeeper as to any other player.

Goalkeeper's Pads:

Goalkeeper's pads vary in size and shape. They should cover the leg from the thigh down to and over the instep. For added protection to her ankles and insteps, the goalkeeper should wear kicking pads or kickers, which should be light in weight and not cumbersome.

Shoes and Socks:

The goalkeeper's shoes should be sturdy, deep-cleated, leather shoes with blocked toes, well-padded along the sides, and with room inside for an extra pair of socks. Rubber sponges are often used on the ankle or instep to absorb shocks. A goalie boot in the form of a half shoe to fit over any flat shoe or sneaker, or canvas kickers with rubber inset to take the shock of kicking, may be used. Whatever type a goalkeeper chooses, the straps should be firm and fit comfortably.

Uniform:

In cool weather, the goalkeeper should be dressed in clothes which will not interfere with her movements. Warm, winter underwear, slacks or warm-up or ski pants, a light windbreaker under a long wool sweater, and gloves will be found essential.

Equipment for Junior Players:

Many youngsters start, at the fourth-grade level, to learn the fundamental principles of the game through relays. A description of the suitable length and weight of the stick may be found in the chart on page 7. Shinguards, goalkeeper equipment, goal pads, and kickers may be purchased in small, medium, and large sizes to fit any player.

The Field

The regulation playing field is rectangular, 90 to 100 yards long and 50 to 60 yards wide. The 100-yard by 60-yard field should be used whenever possible. Junior players should play on a field 85 yards by 45 yards.

FIG. 7. The field and its dimensions.

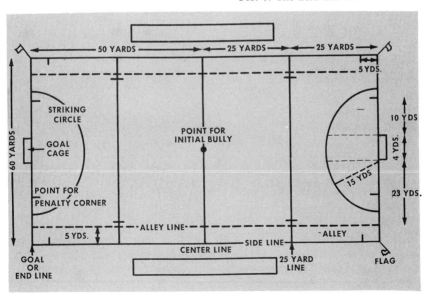

Boundary Lines:

The field is marked with two-inch-wide white lines. The longer lines —those running the length of the field—are called the *side lines;* the shorter lines—those running across the ends of the field—are called the *goal lines,* or *end lines.* The field is divided into four parts by lines parallel to the goal lines; the middle line is the *center line,* or *fifty-yard line,* and the other two lines are the *twenty-five yard lines* (twenty-five yards from the goal lines). In many instances these are marked only for seven yards parallel to the end line and not across the field.

Five-Yard Lines:

The five-yard lines are broken lines that run parallel to and five yards from the side lines for the length of the field. The space between the side line and the five-yard line is called the *alley.*

Goals:

The goals are placed in the center of each goal line, and consist of two perpendicular posts, four yards apart (inside measurement), joined together by a horizontal crossbar, seven feet from the ground. The posts and crossbar should be two inches wide and not more than three inches in depth. The side of the posts and crossbar facing the field should be flat. Posts and crossbars should be painted white. These posts are an aid to a player when shooting a goal. A cord net enclosing this space should be fastened to the posts and crossbar, close to the ground.

Striking Circles:

Directly in front of each goal is a striking circle. A white line, four yards long and fifteen yards from the goal line, is made parallel to the goal line. This line is continued each way to meet the goal line by quarter circles. The goalposts are used as the center for making the quarter circles. The circle meets the goal line fifteen yards from the goalposts. The space enclosed by these lines, and the lines themselves, are called the *striking circle.*

Flags:

Flags four feet high may be placed at the four corners of the playing field to indicate the end lines. These markers help the players to know how far they have to go, how hard to hit the ball, and, on a through pass (ball passed into a space between two opponents) to the wings, help to indicate the direction of the pass. The colors of these flags should be bright. Sometimes school colors are used at one end and visiting team colors are used at the other. The flags should be secured to the flagposts by a hem which can be slipped over the post so that they may be removed easily for cleaning.

Description of the Game

Duration:

A game may be between thirty and sixty minutes in length, divided into two equal periods. That is, the playing period may be adjusted to meet the age and strength of the players and the weather conditions. The *half-time* period is not less than five nor more than ten minutes. It is strongly urged that the length of halves for junior play be shortened; however, fifteen-minute halves may be played.

Officials:

There are two umpires, who are responsible for the control of the game, two official scorekeepers, and two official timekeepers. The umpires should hold a rating for official games; the scorekeepers and timers do not need a rating. A description of how to become an official, as well as how to obtain services of a rated official, may be found in the current Field Hockey – Lacrosse Guide, which should be in the possession of each official, coach, and player.

The Play:

Field hockey is a goal game played between two teams of eleven players each: five forwards (forward line players, attack players, offense players), three halfbacks, two fullbacks, and a goalkeeper (backfield players, defense players).

At the start of the game and after a goal is made, the teams are lined up on either half of the field facing each other; after half-time, teams change ends.

The area from the center line to the goal line is called the *defensive half* by the team that is defending its own goal in that end of the field; the same area is called the *attacking half* by the opponents.

Each team has attack players and defense players. The team that is in possession of the ball is the attacking team or is "on the attack"; it attacks the opponent's goal. The team that does not have possession of the ball and tries to gain possession is the defending team or is "on the defense"; it defends its own goal.

Play begins from a center bully. A bully is the technique used by one player from each team to start the game at the beginning of each half and after a goal is made. Each player has an equal chance to gain possession of the ball. (See page 86.)

The purpose of the game is to score more goals than the opponent and to prevent the opponent from scoring. In order to score a goal the ball must be hit, or must glance off the stick of an attacking player, from within the striking circle, and it must go over the end line between the goalposts.

The successful scoring of goals depends on individual skill, team combination, and knowledge and understanding of the proposed plan of attack. The attacking players try to defeat, by play and by plan, the defending players. The attacking team, by means of passes between players, tries to get the ball down the field to the opponent's striking circle and shoot for goal.

FIG. 8. A goal.

Field hockey is a fast moving game; there are not many fouls to stop the play or to slow it down. A game would be stopped by officials only under the following circumstances:

1. Foul—any infringement of rules by the players. For example:
   a. Pushing—any personal contact.
   b. Holding, hooking—interfering in any way with the opponent's stick. (See Figure 9.)

FIG. 9. Foul—stepping on opponent's stick.

FIG. 10. Foul—obstruction.

c. Obstruction—obstructing the opponent by player's placing her-self between the opponent and the ball. (See Figure 10.)

d. Sticks—raising any part of the stick above the shoulders either at the beginning or at the end of a stroke, or stopping the ball. See Figures 11 and 12.)

e. Handling the ball—using the hands on the ball except to stop it. A raised ball (any ball in the air) may be caught or stopped with the open hand, provided the ball falls as perpendicular as possible. (See Figure 13.)

FIG. 11. Foul—"sticks."

FIG. 12. "Sticks in the rear."

FIG. 13. Using hand to stop raised ball.

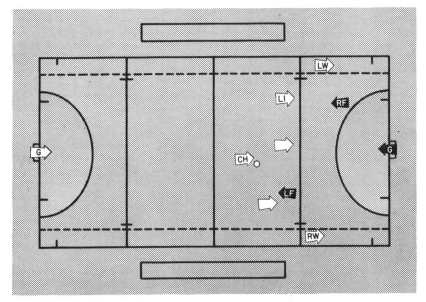

Fɪɢ. 14. Both wings are in an offside position.

   f. Offside—no player is allowed to maneuver ahead of the ball when one of her teammates has possession of it, unless she is in her own half of the field or there are three opponents between her and the goal she is attacking. (See Figure 14.)

2. Out of bounds—whenever the ball goes out over the side line or end line.

3. Accidents or interference with the game.

2

This chapter will illustrate the skills necessary for the successful performance of the important plays in field hockey. *Performance* (use and analysis) shows the need for *Pointers to be stressed in Practice* (drills, skills, or games) for better *Performance*. Thus, we have the full circle which will lead to the art of expert play. (See page 19.)

Each technique described is followed by *Pointers:* "A GOOD PLAYER DOES NOT—A GOOD PLAYER DOES." Correct directions are shown for each fault mentioned. Chapters 3 and 4 show the use of strategy in game play; Chapter 5 shows the play for each position. The final chapter suggests *Practice* drills and games which, if well used, will lead to increased skill. *"Better Performance, through valuable Pointers, stressed in well-directed Practice"* is a method by which hockey players, both beginners and experts, may continue to improve their game.

The Art of Success
in Strokes, Dodges, Tackles

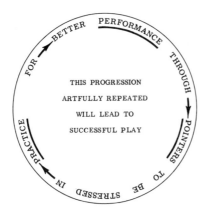

Teachers play a key role in the improvement of hockey. The objectives of a good coach are to give the beginning player a thorough grounding and a genuine interest in the game, to enable the intermediate player to improve her play, and to develop in the experienced player initiative to increase her skills and to achieve peak performance in creative and expert play.

The foundation for creative hockey players can be laid in beginning classes through clear explanation and skillful demonstration of the *how, when, where,* and *why* of the game.

Stickwork involved in any game should be thoroughly practiced before it becomes the groundwork of competition. All the helpful ideas in the world are of little value without the technical skill to carry them through. Sometimes players fail to make progress because they have not really understood how to perform properly the precise movements of the stick and body for receiving and controlling a pass on the run; the particular footwork involved in driving, shooting, or passing on the run; and scores of special techniques without which real skill will be lacking. Increased practice *itself* will not lead inevitably to better performance; the practice must follow a pattern of well-directed coaching hints and suggestions. These are included as "pointers" in the following pages.

The joy of playing hockey, as of any game, will come through skilled, competitive play. With well-directed practice, beginners who are mastering such fundamentals as handling of the stick, stopping the ball, dribbling, and driving, can enjoy the learning of each technique. The various methods of dodging and tackling can then be developed, leading eventually to full knowledge, skill, and the genuine thrill of competitive game play. A dodge is the means by which to evade a tackling opponent. A tackle is the means by which a player takes the ball away from her opponent and gains control of it. The best time to tackle is the instant the ball is out of the opponent's control. The choice of stroke, dodge, or tackle is determined by: (1) the positions of the two players relative to other players; whether the tackling player is approaching or overtaking the player with the ball; and (2) the speed and control of the two players involved.

Following are descriptions of the fundamental techniques necessary to early development of basic skills. It should be noted that the techniques might be presented in varying ways and orders of progression, both for the personal-use learner and for the teacher of field hockey. However, the following sequence has been found, through much use with learners and teachers of the sport, to be especially effective.

How to Hold and Carry the Stick

THE GRIP

Use:

The grip is used to hold the stick, and it varies according to the strokes used.

Performance:

With the left hand, grasp the handle of the stick at the top, as though shaking hands with it; place the right hand close to and below the left. Take a firm grip with both hands. (The V's made by the thumb and forefinger of each hand should be one directly above the other, on the front of the handle.) Assume a comfortable stance, with knees slightly bent and body in as upright a position as possible. Place the stick perpendicular to the ground with the tip straight forward. The flat side of the stick, the left shoulder, and the feet should face the direction in which the ball is to go.

Note: "Hands together" enables a player to get the benefit of full leverage.

TWO-HAND CARRY

Use:

The two-hand carry is used to hold the stick while running to get into position or to play the ball.

FIG. 15. The grip.   FIG. 16. Two-hand carry.

FIG. 17. The stick will not impede your progress if you allow it to swing naturally with your arms and make it a part of you.

Performance:

Grasp the handle of the stick at the top with the left hand. The right hand, which is cupped with palm facing forward, holds the weight of the stick. Bend the elbows comfortably, take a loose grip, and hold the stick horizontally across the body, waist high, with the toe of the stick facing up.

Note: In this position, the stick should swing easily with the motion of running.

Bring the stick into play by dropping the blade of the stick forward toward the ground and slipping the right hand up on the handle close to the left. Hands should be one to two inches apart.

ONE-HAND CARRY

Use:

The one-hand carry is used to hold the stick while the player is running to get into position or to play the ball. This carry is one of readiness and anticipation for immediate and subsequent play of the ball. It should not be used often while the player is running a distance at top speed.

Performance:

Grasp the stick with the left hand at the top. The blade of the stick, which almost touches the ground, faces the direction of the oncoming ball. As the ball approaches, reach with the right hand to play the ball. Keep the eyes on the ball.

Note: The one-hand carry is preferred by some players. They feel that by using it they have a better chance to get the stick on the ball, as the stick is already close to the ground, lessening the degree of error in fielding the ball.

Pointers for Carrying the Stick:

A GOOD PLAYER:

DOES NOT	BUT ⟶ DOES
1. Shift the left hand on the stick. By shifting the top hand, she would not have the blade in proper position for making any stroke on the ball.	1. Keep the left hand in the same position for all strokes, so that she will know where the face of her stick is.

2. Let the stick hang loosely at her side or allow it to drag in back, as she would then be unprepared for fast action.

2. Hold the stick extended slightly forward, free of the feet, keeping the head of the stick close to the ground, ready to bring it into action in a split second if necessary.

3. Remain tense, as tenseness brings on unnecessary fatigue.

3. Remain alert, eager, and ready to go. She relaxes when not immediately involved in the play, having learned to relax physically but to stay alert mentally.

4. Hold her stick rigidly, as to do so would prevent a natural, easy motion.

4. Have a relaxed grip on the stick, in order to prevent awkwardness, undue tension, and fatigue.

THE DRIBBLE

Use:

The dribble is used to advance or move the ball forward when running with it. A player may use a close dribble or a loose dribble.

Performance:

Place the left hand at the top of the handle of the stick, the back of the hand facing forward. With the right hand, grasp the handle two or three inches below the left with palm forward. Thumbs are around the stick for a firmer grip.

Keep arms and stick slightly to the right and ahead of the body. Bend the elbows. This will allow the stick to meet the ball almost at a perpendicular; it will also allow for freedom in activity.

The head is in one position at all times, and eyes are on the ball, which is a few inches ahead of the leading foot and slightly to the right of the body, enabling the player to run freely. Hit the ball with the flat side of the stick, which faces forward. A free and easy wrist motion is used to hit the ball with short successive taps. This constitutes a push with the right hand and a pull with the left.

Tap the ball when weight is on the forward foot. The ball should be tapped as hard as is necessary to keep it in front of the forward foot. It is kept close to the stick to prevent the opponent from taking it. Run with short, quick steps. Look up to determine the position of teammates and opponents in relation to self. Consider what and where the next play will be.

Note: Dribble with the stick close to the ball. This control of the ball gives an opportunity to pass at any moment, and also provides less chance for the opponent to take the ball away.

Close dribbling requires diligent practice. The unskilled dribbler will kick or overrun the ball more often than she will hit it.

THE LOOSE DRIBBLE

Use:

The loose dribble is used when there is a clear field ahead and no opponent is near enough to tackle or intercept. It is sometimes used to tease the opponent: the dribbler allows her opponent to come toward the ball, makes her think she can get it, and then passes it out of her opponent's reach.

Performance:

Hit the ball and run up to it, instead of keeping it close to the stick. Tap the ball hard, making the ball roll farther ahead of the stick than in the close dribble.

Note: Loose dribbling permits a player to move fast. One can run more quickly when not trying to manage or control the ball; however, loose dribbling gives an opponent a better chance to gain possession of the ball.

Fig. 18. The dribble (side view).

Fig. 19. The dribble (front view).

Pointers for the Dribble:

A GOOD PLAYER:

DOES NOT	BUT ——▶ DOES
1. Tap the ball so hard or so far ahead that it gives the opponent a better opportunity to gain possession of the ball.	1. Tap the ball as hard as necessary to keep it in front of her and close to her stick.
2. Get the ball too far out on the right side. This would cause her to reach and bend too much at the waist, slowing her up.	2. Keep her body position almost upright and the ball ahead and slightly to the right, free of the feet, with the stick in a perpendicular position.
3. Raise her stick too high off the ground. This would prevent the execution of a quick pass or it might allow an opponent to take the ball away from her.	3. Keep her stick close to the ground and close behind the ball for good ball control.

FIG. 20. The dribble. Keep the ball ahead and close to your stick.

FIG. 21. Loose dribble—when you have a clear field ahead and no opponent is near enough to tackle.

4. Get the ball on her left side and then use a reverse stick.

4. Move her feet to get back into position if the ball is on her left side.

Drives

STRAIGHT DRIVE

Use:

The straight drive is a hard stroke used for passing, shooting, or clearing.

Performance:

Keep the left arm close to the body and the right arm out to the side with elbows bent slightly and wrists cocked; the head of the stick should be about waist high. Body weight is back on the left or right foot. Keep the back leg straight, but do not lock the knee.

Drag the stick straight back along the ground.

The head should not move. Relax—don't lock neck or shoulders.

The ball is in a position ahead, opposite the forward foot.

Note: The reason for bending the elbows is to prevent "sticks." (See page 15.)

In starting the stick on the forward, downward swing, extend and straighten both arms and uncock the wrists with a snap as the stick meets the ball in the center of the blade.

26

FIG. 22. Drive: back
swing and beginning of
the forward swing (Part
1).

FIG. 23. Drive: forward
swing and moment of
contact (Part 2).

FIG. 24. Drive: follow- through (Part 3).

FIG. 25. Good follow-through of drive and a good "going" position, i.e. ready to follow up and keep on the attack.

Keep wrists firm. There should be a gradual shift of weight from the back to the forward foot with the downward, forward swing of the stick. Body weight behind the ball adds force to the stroke.

The forward knee is bent; back leg is extended; back heel is off the ground. Shoulders turn naturally and head remains in one position.

Head of stick moves straight forward, like an arrow pointing toward the target, which will give the ball direction. Extend arms and stick as far as possible in the direction of the shot. Maintain firm wrists. The stick should go straight back with the flat side facing the ball. Swing the stick forward in the direction in which the ball is to go.

Force, speed of execution, and accuracy are the major points to be emphasized for this stroke.

Pointers for the Straight Drive:

A GOOD PLAYER:

DOES NOT	BUT ⟶ DOES
1. Lift her head. This would cause her to top the ball, hit behind it, or miss it completely.	1. Keep her eyes on the ball.
2. Fail to hit the ball squarely.	2. Hit the ball in the center of the blade.
3. Hit the ball when it is too close to her, making the hit inaccurate, slow, and lacking in force.	3. Hit the ball when it is diagonally opposite the front foot.

RIGHT DRIVE

Use:

For a hard shot or pass to the right, the right drive is necessary for most players.

Performance:

The position of hands and the grip are the same as for the straight drive. Before beginning this stroke, the right foot should be forward, with the toes pointing straight ahead. The ball should be to the right side, behind the rear foot. Bend knees slightly. Rotate or twist the upper body well to the right. Swing the stick behind, taking the right shoulder back and pointing the left shoulder in the direction of the intended pass or hit. This allows the stick to swing from behind the hips and toward the ball. Cock the wrists. Keep the head in one position (independent of the body twist), and keep eyes over the ball.

At the moment of impact, the head is set and does not move, eyes look over the ball, knees are easy, and arms are extended. Left hand leads. The right hand and arm give the power behind the stick. The weight shifts to the front foot and wrists uncock as the face of the stick hits the ball squarely.

Fig. 26. Right drive: beginning of the back swing (Part 1).

FIG. 27. Right drive: moment of impact (Part 2).

FIG. 28. Right drive: follow-through (Part 3).

During the follow-through the head remains in the same position. Extend arms and stick. Shift weight completely to the front foot. Only after the ball is hit does the back leg move forward.

The flat surface of the stick faces the direction of the ball.

Important: Acceleration of the head of the stick should continue right through the swing with a full reach.

While running, continue to get the feet a little ahead of the ball, then lift the stick, twist the body, and with a quick, crisp hit whip the ball hard across the field.

The right drive is a very difficult shot to execute well when running, because the ball must be behind the player before the stroke is made. The back swing must be started soon enough to permit the forward swing as the ball is approaching. Slow timing on the hit causes ineffective drives. If a player slows down at all, her opponent may thwart her. This is the stroke a left wing *must* practice.

Pointers for the Right Drive:

A GOOD PLAYER:

DOES NOT	BUT ⟶ DOES
1. Look up too soon.	1. Keep her head steady, with her eyes on the ball.
2. Shift her weight so soon that she makes an out-of-control shot which would result in a dangerous, undercut ball.	2. Move her back foot forward after the ball is hit.
3. Turn her toes to the right as she rotates her upper body when preparing to drive.	3. Keep her toes pointed straight ahead when she drives the ball to the right, in order to avoid giving away the direction of her pass, neither slowing up the play nor permitting an interception by the defense.

LEFT DRIVE

Use:

The left drive is used to pass the ball to the left, and is stronger and more widely used than the right drive.

Performance:

The position of hands and grip is the same as for the straight drive.

When making a hit or drive to the left, place the ball in front of the body, either by a tap to the left to get it in the correct position for the hit or by moving the feet around to the right. The weight is on either foot behind the stroke and the stick is perpendicular to the ground with the blade facing to the left.

Pointers for the Left Drive:

A GOOD PLAYER:

DOES NOT	BUT ⟶ DOES
1. Top or miss the ball, or dig up the ground.	1. Keep her eyes on the ball until it is actually hit.
2. Pass weakly.	2. Pass with precision and decision.

WRIST DRIVE

Use:

This shot is used when there is not sufficient time for a full swing in a straight drive or for a quick, short pass. It is a very useful shot in an emergency.

Performance:

The position of the hands for the wrist drive is the same as for the straight drive. In the swing to hit the ball, move the stick back a few inches only and use a snap of the wrists to contact the ball.

Pointers for the Wrist Drive:

A GOOD PLAYER:

DOES NOT	BUT ⟶ DOES
1. Use a full swing.	1. Use powerful wrist action to execute this stroke.
2. Take too much time when executing this stroke.	2. Execute this stroke quickly.

Fielding and Controlling the Ball

There are two methods for stopping the ball—with the stick and with the hand. The stick is the easiest and fastest method to use.

STICK-STOP—BALL CONTROL IN FIELDING

Use:

The stick-stop is used to stop a ball. When the ball is stopped, it should be under control and in such a position that player may either pass the ball to another or shoot for goal immediately.

Performance:

Step forward, with the weight over the forward foot, whether it be left or right, and with both knees slightly bent. Slide the right hand down the handle about two or three inches below the top left hand. With left hand and arm leading and left elbow up and out, place the stick, with flat surface forward, perpendicular to and on the ground directly behind the path of the ball. The left-hand grip must be firm throughout. The right-hand grip should be loose enough to allow the stick to "give" in the direction from which the ball is coming. When the desired position has been reached, secure a firm grip on the stick with the right hand.

There must be a "give" at the moment of contact, to stop the ball dead against the stick or to keep the ball close. In order to do this, let the stick touch the ground behind the ball, and then pull the stick back; otherwise the ball will get too far forward and out of control. Good fielding means perfect control of the ball from the moment it touches the stick until it is passed or played.

Fig. 29. Preparing to stop the ball (side view).

Fig. 30. Stopping the ball
(front view).

Fig. 31. Good fielding—ball under control. Notice the ball on the player's stick.

Pointers for the Stick-Stop:

A GOOD PLAYER:

DOES NOT	BUT ⟶ DOES
1. Wait for the ball to come to her.	1. Run to meet the ball.
2. Relax her attention.	2. Concentrate—an alert mind gives her a better chance to control the ball and avoid having it intercepted. She keeps on the attack.
3. Hold the stick directly in front of her feet. The ball would rebound forward and the hit would be slowed because there would be no room for the back swing. If the ball were not properly stopped, it would hit the feet or shins and bound forward, which is a foul.	3. Hold the stick well out in front and slightly to the right side so that the body will be in the proper relationship to the ball to get off a good hit. This placement of the stick eliminates any chance of tripping over it.
4. Hold the handle of the stick sloped backward because the ball, when making contact with the blade, would go over the stick and roll behind her. A stick in this position is apt to cause a lifted ball in the direction of a player's face.	4. Push her left hand well forward, keeping the blade slightly closed.
5. Put her stick down at the last minute, or too late.	5. Put her stick down on the ground long before she thinks it is necessary.
6. Jab into the ball, making it rebound forward out of control.	6. "Give" with the stick to control the ball, placing it in position to be hit again.

HAND STOP

Use:

The hand stop is seldom used because players must have plenty of time to clear the ball after stopping it. Some players use it to stop a corner hit (see page 109), because there is less chance of the ball bounding off the stick. The hand is often used to stop a lofted ball that is above shoulder height.

Performance:

When the ball rolls on the ground, the player places herself directly behind the ball. Holding the stick in the left hand by the side, bend the knees, lean forward, and place the right hand in front of the right foot, with the right wrist on the ground. As the ball hits the palm of the hand, close the fingers around the ball in order to stop it. Then stand up and place both hands on the stick. Either drive the ball away or step aside and let a team player hit the ball.

Note: This requires a little more time than the stick stop. The ball must be rendered motionless. It must not be advanced.

When the ball is lofted above shoulder height, catch it in the hand and drop it immediately so that it falls perpendicularly to the ground.

Pointers for the Hand Stop:

A GOOD PLAYER:

DOES NOT	BUT ⟶ DOES
1. Let the ball rebound forward from her hand.	1. Stop the ball motionless.
2. Use the hand stop often.	2. Occasionally use the hand stop on a corner. (See page 109.)

STRAIGHT TACKLE

Use:

This tackle is used when an opponent, using a loose dribble, is running directly toward the player.

FIG. 32. Straight tackle.

FIG. 33. Fullback tackles the center forward.

Performance:

The tackler moves straight toward the ball rather than approaching it at an angle.

Place the stick toward the ball and close to the ground several feet before the point at which you expect to meet the ball. Keep the eyes on the ball every second in order to anticipate the next move. Move quickly to the left or right to keep in direct line with the ball. At the moment the tackle is made, place the stick directly in front of the oncoming ball, bend the body, and have the body balance slightly forward to keep the blade from going back; otherwise, the ball will bounce over the stick.

The left hand is well away from the body and the right hand is placed loosely on the stick to allow a little "give."

Pointers for the Straight Tackle:

A GOOD PLAYER:

DOES NOT	BUT ⟶ DOES
1. Set her stick in front of her opponent.	1. Get her stick in the path of the ball.
2. Slant her stick back, allowing the ball to jump over the stick.	2. Keep the top of her stick well forward and away from her body.
3. Hold her stick up off the ground. If the stick is up, the opponent can put the ball under the stick.	3. Keep her stick on the ground throughout the tackle. This makes ball control possible.

37

DOES NOT	BUT ⟶ DOES
4. Place herself in a weak defensive position permitting her opponent to get by her easily.	4. Get herself into a position opposite the opponent whom she plans to tackle.

PUSH STROKE

Use:

The player uses the push stroke for a short distance pass. It is a quick, easy pass, without the danger of fouling, when there is no need, time, or space for a hard drive. It may be executed at any moment, and in any direction, while the player runs at full speed.

Fig. 34. Start of the push stroke.

Performance:

Grasp the top of the stick firmly as described for the dribble. Bend the left elbow high, and place it well in front of the body; the right elbow should be out and away from the body to help support the stick and give accuracy to the pass.

Hold the stick perpendicular to the ground with the flat side touching the ball and the handle slightly farther away from the body than the blade.

Begin with the weight on the back foot and transfer it as the stroke is made. The ball should be slightly to the right and in front of the forward foot.

The stroke starts with the ball against the blade of the stick. There is no back swing. Push the stick forward with the right hand: while straightening the right arm. Pull back on the stick with the left hand, thus using the stick as a lever. The right hand acts as a pivot and also as a guide to prevent the stick from rising any higher than the knee. Tighten both wrists (using very little wrist *action,* as this tends to lift the ball), as the stick is pushed along the ground in the direction of the pass. The stick is kept in contact with the ball as long as possible—sweeping the ball forward along the ground. At the finish of the stroke, the arms, stick, and body are extended forward in full reach.

Pointers for the Push Stroke:

A Good Player:

DOES NOT	BUT ──────▶ DOES
1. Keep the ball close to her feet. If she did this, she would have no force in her stroke; therefore, she would not be able to direct the ball well.	1. Keep the ball to the right side diagonally in front of the forward foot.
2. Slap at the ball, which would make for a slower stroke, and create a possibility for the opponent to rob the ball.	2. Start with her stick directly on the ball. This play allows her to pass it immediately without losing either time or the ball.
3. Raise her stick above her knee as she finishes the stroke.	3. Keep her stick close to the ground, gaining more accuracy and resulting in a shot which will be easier for her team player to field.

THE PULL TO THE LEFT DODGE

Use:

The pull to the left dodge may be used to evade an oncoming tackling opponent.

Performance:

As the opponent comes in to tackle, move to the left with the ball.

Both the ball and the feet move to the left at the same time. As the player executes this dodge, she checks her forward motion in order to move sideways. Turn the blade of the stick to the left, maintaining contact with the ball. Give the ball a series of taps to the side, never allowing it to get to the left side. When player is out of reach of her opponent, she is in a position to play the ball.

Note: Quick movements with the feet and the action of the wrists are the vital points. The right wrist which works at the start of the pull to the left is followed immediately by the left wrist movement to get the ball out in front.

FIG. 35. Beginning of the pull to the left dodge (Part 1).

FIG. 36. Finish of the pull to the left dodge (Part 2).

Pointers for the Pull to the Left Dodge:

A GOOD PLAYER:

DOES NOT	BUT ⟶ DOES
1. Cross her legs, get off balance, or hit the ball out of her own control.	1. Have good footwork, control of her body, and the ability to move quickly and efficiently in all directions.
2. Make her first motion too soon or too late.	2. Have a well-timed dodge to evade the tackling opponent.

LEFT-HAND LUNGE

Use:

The left-hand lunge should be used when the tackler has been passed and the dribbler is being chased on the tackler's left. Its purpose is to stop or deflect the ball. The lunge may also be used as a pass to a team player when an extra reach is needed to get the ball. It is used occasionally to keep a diagonal pass from going over the side line or goal line.

Performance:

While running, use the two-hand carry position. Allow enough distance from the opponent for an extended reach. This play enables a player to take her opponent by surprise. Keep stick at waist level when swinging stick backward in order to avoid making "sticks."

As player lunges, she must push her stick forward across the body, release the right hand, and fling it backward to aid body balance. The left arm, with a firm wrist, extends as far as possible; the body bends well forward; and the head of the stick travels downward to the ground as it makes contact with the ball.

As soon as the stick contacts the ball, it is used as a pivotal point to bring the body around. Bring back foot forward, and pivot to the left. Replace right hand on the handle of the stick and swing body weight behind the stick. Proceeding in the direction from which she came, player keeps the ball under control. The ball may be caught between both sticks. Use a quick upward movement and lift the ball over opponent's stick.

A player must learn to judge the distance covered by her own lunges, and allow ample room for execution. If she gets too close, she will lack reach and strength. Aim slightly ahead of the ball for better timing and accuracy. The left-hand lunge must be accurate, strong, and well controlled to avoid tripping or hitting the legs or stick of opponent. The blade of the stick must meet the ball squarely, or an undercut will result. Good judgment and strong left wrists are necessary.

Fig. 37. Start of the Left-hand lunge (Part 1).

Fig. 38. Left-hand lunge: contact with the ball (Part 2).

FIG. 39. Left-hand lunge: end of tackle (Part 3).

FIG. 40. Start of Left-hand lunge. Player holds her stick in a relaxed position, using a wide sweeping motion.

Fig. 41. Left-hand lunge may be used to stop the ball. Allow ample room for execution. It must be accurate and well controlled.

Pointers for the Left-Hand Lunge:

A Good Player:

| DOES NOT | BUT ⟶ DOES |

1. Use a choppy motion—upward and downward—making "sticks."

2. Hold her stick higher than her waist at the start of the lunge.

3. Get too close to her opponent, resulting in a weak lunge with no control.

4. Lift her stick off the ground before regaining control with right hand and facing opponent. To do so would allow opponent to control the ball, as there would be no opposition.

5. Hit the ball backward into her opponent—a dangerous play.

1. Hold her stick in a relaxed position just below the waist, using a wide sweeping motion.

2. Keep her stick at waist level at the start of the lunge to avoid "sticks."

3. Use a good reach, with arm and stick fully extended away from opponent.

4. Keep her stick on the ground until she turns her body around in the direction from which she came replacing her right hand on her stick in a straight-tackle position.

5. Hit the ball so that it goes sideways. This is done by facing the position of the blade in the direction the ball is to go.

6. Get close to the ball. Such poor timing would result in a badly directed, half-topped, weak, or slow deflection.

6. Time her firm, crisp hit when the ball is off the opponent's stick; otherwise, she is apt to hit the ground before the ball, or might hit the opponent's stick or shins.

THE FLICK

Use:

The flick, a reaching stroke, is used for passes or for shots at goal.

Performance:

Grasp the top of the handle of the stick with the left hand, as for the dribble. Body is in a semi-crouched position. Crouching the body and knees gives more power behind the stroke. Weight is balanced between the toes of the rear foot and all of the front foot.

The ball should be well to the right and diagonally ahead of the forward foot. This play requires the player to bend and extend her reach.

Rest the stick on the ground, with the face of the stick behind the ball. There is no backswing to start the stroke. Simultaneously, pull the stick toward the body with the left hand and push away with the right hand, snap the wrists, and push forcefully from back foot. This play will give added force and momentum to the ball and raise it from the ground.

Fig. 42. The flick: start (Part 1).

FIG. 43. The flick: follow-through (Part 2).

This stroke has a great deal of snap and more force than the push pass. With strong, quick, wrist work the flick can have great force and the ball will travel far if necessary. Emphasis should be placed on accuracy, speed, and skill.

FIG. 44. Flick: start of the stroke. Extra crouch of body and knees gives more power behind the stroke.

FIG. 45. Lovely execution of the flick. Ball going over opponent's stick and levelling off for team player to pick up.

Pointers for the Flick:

A GOOD PLAYER:

DOES NOT	BUT ⟶ DOES
1. Start with the ball close to her feet, unable to execute enough force to lift the ball from the ground.	1. Start with the ball well to the right side and diagonally ahead of the front foot for more force and power to the stroke.
2. Hit wildly.	2. Use a flick when players are closely marked (see page 73), to vary her play.

RIGHT DODGE–THE PUSH TO THE RIGHT

Use:

The push to the right dodge is used to evade an oncoming tackling opponent.

Performance:

As the opponent comes in to tackle, the player must change speed as she pushes or taps the ball to the non-stick side of her opponent, then move to her opponent's stick side.

Recovering the ball as soon as possible behind her opponent who has been passed and has overrun the ball, she continues forward with the ball. It should go as little out of control as possible, so that it is never far out of line for the opposing team to recover and no time or energy is wasted.

Fig. 46. Right dodge: Fig. 47. Right dodge:
start (Part 1).   completion (Part 2).

Fig. 48. Right dodge: player cutting around opponent without any
waste of time or space, while opponent is off balance, to regain control of the ball, thus completing a successful dodge.

Pointers for the Right Dodge:

A GOOD PLAYER:

DOES NOT	BUT ⟶ DOES
1. Dodge too soon, as her opponent would have a better chance to gain possession of the ball.	1. Execute this dodge with deception.
2. Push, tap, or hit the ball too hard or so far to the right that she cannot recover it herself.	2. Time her push to the right so that her opponent cannot tackle successfully.

CIRCULAR TACKLE

Use:

The circular tackle is an overtaking tackle used when a player is on her opponent's left.

Performance:

In order to execute this stroke, player overtakes (is slightly ahead of) the opponent at the beginning of the tackle. As player's body is coming around, the left shoulder and left wrist lead and the right shoulder is back. She continues in this way until facing opponent in a straight tackle position. The stick is on the ground as player comes shoulder to shoulder with opponent; the blade continually faces the ball.

FIG. 49. Getting into position for a circular tackle.

FIG. 50. Note that the player leads with her left shoulder when making the turn. She must make the tackle when the ball is off the stick and ahead of her opponent.

Having completed the tackle, and with the ball on the stick, player is then in a position to do what she wants to do with the ball—pass, shoot, dribble, put into a space, or whatever the situation demands.

Note: The blade of the stick literally traces an elongated "J" on the ground in doing the circular tackle.

Pointers for a Circular Tackle:

A GOOD PLAYER:

DOES NOT	BUT ────▶ DOES
1. Obstruct.	1. Lead with her left shoulder in making the turn, keeping the right shoulder well back, which necessitates her running faster than her opponent.
2. Have poor balance, impeding a good tackle.	2. Have good footwork and good body control.

SCOOP

Use:

The scoop stroke is a shoveling or lifting stroke used as a dodge, and is sometimes used as a shot for a goal or as a short pass; it is also useful on heavy, wet grounds.

Performance:

The left hand is at the top of the stick. The right hand is two or three inches below the left. Lay the blade of the stick back.

To lift the ball, push the stick gently forward and upward with both hands and shift the weight to the front foot. This *must* be gradual and gentle. If a quick and jerky stroke is used the stick will go under the ball. Keep the knees straight, and follow through with back leg as the ball is scooped into the air. At the completion of the stroke, the blade of the stick is about knee high. The ball should be raised only a few inches from the ground. As opponent comes in to tackle, scoop the ball (at the crucial moment) into a clear space ahead and continue forward with the ball.

Note: Lay the blade of the stick well back before scooping if the ball is to be lifted. Beginners tend to push forward too forcefully and too quickly, and as a result the ball rolls back over the stick.

Fig. 51. The scoop: start of the stroke.

Pointers for the Scoop:

A GOOD PLAYER:

DOES NOT	BUT ⟶ DOES
1. Stand in an upright position, as this would prevent her from being able to lift the ball.	1. Get into a semi-crouched position in order to lift the ball.
2. Scoop the ball too far ahead allowing it to get out of control and go to an opponent.	2. *Gently* scoop the ball by not being too forceful in the execution of the stroke.

REVERSE

Use:

The reverse stroke is used as a pass or a dodge.

Performance:

Grasp the stick with the left hand at the top. Reverse the stick in the hands by rotating the left hand to the left, letting the stick slide in a loose hand until the toe of the stick points down. The right hand then re-grips the stick, placing the flat side of the stick against the ball facing to the right. The reverse can be done without change of grip. Reverse the stick by turning the wrists over rather than by turning the handle in a grasp, and extend the arms. The body is upright and the head is down. Body weight is over the forward foot as the stick swings from the left to the right. Use a short backswing and follow-through, hitting the ball with the toe of the stick.

Pointers for the Reverse Stroke:

A GOOD PLAYER:

DOES NOT	BUT ⟶ DOES
1. Obstruct with her shoulder, arm, or body in an effort to play the ball.	1. Adjust her body position so that the ball is always played when it is in front of her body.
2. Use this stroke—unless there is not enough time to get herself around the ball.	2. Use this stroke only in an emergency.

REVERSE-TO-THE-RIGHT DODGE

Use:

The reverse-to-the-right dodge is used when a player dribbling the ball is about to be tackled from behind by an opponent who is preparing to use the left-hand lunge.

Performance:

When dribbling the ball, stop "dead" just as opponent is ready to lunge, or is lunging, and quickly reverse the stick, drawing it a short distance across to the opponent's non-stick side (tap the ball to the right or backward). Due to the sudden stop, the would-be tackler overruns the ball, and dodger has the time to make an unimpeded pass to a team player or across the field.

Accurate dodging requires timing, control, speed, deception, and good footwork.

Pointers for Pull to the Right with Reverse Stick:

A GOOD PLAYER:

DOES NOT	BUT ⟶ DOES
1. Hit the ball loosely and to the side, and then run to get the uncontrolled ball. This would allow her opponent to get the ball because it is out of control, and would prevent her from completing the dodge.	1. Tap the ball just hard enough that, with one step to the side, she can pass the ball or shoot for a goal.

REVERSE STICK TACKLE

Use:

The reverse stick tackle is used as a spoil stroke to prevent an opponent from completing her play.

Performance:

Use the reverse stick grasp with a firm hold. Reach forward as far as possible, keeping the elbows straight. Lift the stick back slightly. Place the weight on the forward foot and on the toe of the rear foot. Swing the toe of the stick at the ball, deflecting the ball to the opponent's stick side or to a team player and putting it out of the opponent's reach. Hit the ball with a short, quick, sharp tap and tighten the wrists. Immediately withdraw the stick after contacting the ball, in order to avoid tripping opponent.

The reverse stick tackle may be executed with the right hand in order to provide a player with a longer reach. It must be executed in a manner that will not cause an obstruction by putting the right arm, shoulder, or any part of the body between the opponent and the ball.

Shift the two-hand carrying position of the stick to grip the handle a few inches from the top with the right hand. The left hand is below the right. Reverse the stick so that the toe of the stick points toward the ground. Following a short backswing, throw the stick at the ball with the left hand. Release the left hand and bring the left arm back to the side for better body balance. The right wrist tightens up as the tip of the blade taps the ball.

A player must not touch or obstruct her opponent or hit the opponent's stick before touching the ball. After the tackle is made, change the grip to a dribble or drive grip.

FIG. 52. Reverse stick tackle (two hands).

FIG. 53. Reverse stick tackle (one hand).

FIG. 54. Fullback attempting a reverse stick tackle.

Pointers for the Reverse Stick Tackle:

A GOOD PLAYER:

DOES NOT	BUT ⟶ DOES
1. Get too close to her opponent, as such move might result in fouling.	1. Get well to the side of her opponent, to enable her to use her reach for a stronger, more controlled stroke.
2. Tackle too soon or too late.	2. Have good timing, catching her opponent off balance, or getting the ball when it is far enough off her opponent's stick.
3. Hold her stick across and in front of the body of her opponent, which would cause a foul.	3. Take her stick away quickly.
4. Have a weak grip lacking control of the stick.	4. Have a grip on the stick that is firm enough to get the ball to the right side of the opponent or to a team player.

THE JAB

Use:

The jab stroke is used to get a ball that cannot be reached while both hands are on the stick. It is useful in preventing, temporarily, an opponent from playing the ball. It is a one-handed poke or thrust at the ball, performed with either the left or right hand.

Performance:

Lay the blade of the stick back. Hold the top of the stick firmly, at the top of the handle, with either the left or right hand—wrist on top. The body is upright, and elbow is bent and close to the side.

Bend the body well forward and take a long stride; put the weight onto the forward foot. At the same time, push the stick forward and close to the ground. Extend arm as far as possible, and reach for the ball with the flat side of the stick.

It is better to use the left-hand jab in trying to reach the ball from the non-stick side of an opponent, because the right shoulder can be kept back to lessen the possibility of obstruction.

If the blade of the stick is laid too far back, the ball will roll over it. The jab must be made quickly and accurately. To be successful it has to be timed perfectly; when the opponent's stick comes off the ball as she is dribbling, or, as she is getting ready to drive this stroke can put the ball out of her control. Follow up with another play immediately.

Note: Do not execute this stroke when close to opponent.

Fig. 55. The jab.

FIG. 56. Reach for the ball.

Pointers for the Jab:

A GOOD PLAYER:

DOES NOT	BUT ⟶ DOES
1. Get so close to her opponent as to have to avoid pushing her.	1. Keep her body out of her opponent's way. The opponent should not have to break her stride.
2. Fail to make direct contact with the ball. She avoids hitting the ground with the stick, tripping her opponent, hitting her opponent's stick, or even missing the ball.	2. Have a well-timed, well-directed stroke with excellent control of the stick.

3

Field hockey is not only a game of skill but also a game of science. In addition to having a good knowledge of the game, being able to run fast, and possessing a firm foundation of individual techniques and skills, a player must be willing and able to use her energies and skill for strengthening the team as a whole.

The player's best positioning or course of action is entirely dependent upon the location of the ball and of the other players; this presents so many variations that it is impossible to plot definite plays or to map out a course of action in advance. Each player must rely on her own initiative and intelligence to make her decisions for the particular problem of the moment, and must, at the same time, work in accordance with the proposed plan of attack understood by the whole team. However, in this chapter are suggested a general concept of

Strategy Means "Know How"

58

attack and defense and a comprehensive plan of team combination on which play can be based and from which individual ideas can be expressed, developed, and expanded.

The purposes here are to show proficient use of skills and strategy and to suggest ideas which will encourage players to think for themselves and which may be used as sound concepts for the planning of other team plays.

The accompanying illustrations show actual play as well as a model hockey field with magnetic arrows, to give a clearer idea of the approximate positions of the players and their spacing on the field and to demonstrate a definite technique. Remember that a hockey field is 90–100 yards long and 50–60 yards wide. During many situations, when the game is played on a regulation field, there may be large spaces not covered by any player. Following are descriptions of game situations with varying individual and team strategy possibilities that will lead to the development of real and needed "know how" of the game.

PASSING

Passes between forwards are used to avoid and penetrate the defense and to advance the ball quickly toward the opponents' goal. Passes from the defense players to their forwards should initiate the attack, either as soon as a forward is free or as soon as there is a clear space ahead. Passes between defense players are used only to get out of a difficult situation or to jockey the ball into position for a pass to their forwards. A fellow defense player may be in a better position to pass to a forward because the opponents are closing in fast.

An attack is initiated, carried on, and successfully completed by means of good passing. Players must learn to combine with their team players by using such passes as: long and short, easy and hard, flat (square), or through. Passes may be made in any direction in order to make it difficult for the opponent to intercept (see page 69) or mark (see page 73). Long, hard, through passes are quite successful against defense players who do not cover (see page 76) or back up (see page 71) each other. Direct, quick, deceptive passes are effective against a well-coordinated, covering defense (see page 76).

In making a long, diagonal pass from the left side of the field to the right, the player should place the ball well ahead of the receiver. A receiver on the right side of the field has the advantage of receiving the ball on her stick side and can use an extended reach, if necessary, without a change of pace.

To make a through pass from the right side of the field to the left, the pass should not be as hard as those made from the left to the right. Usually, players on the left side of the field have more difficulty in fielding the ball. A pass made from right to left is directed to the stick (right) side of the receiver. This pass makes it necessary for the player to turn the blade of her stick in order to receive the ball.

A forward line player must choose the openings and help the line get through by means of quick, accurate, and varied passes. A triangular pass, which involves any two players of the same team, is effective if well-timed and accurate. A forward, about to be tackled, makes a short, square pass to a team player, who immediately returns the ball, using a short, diagonal pass. This is most difficult to stop if the forward, about to be tackled, passes to her team player on her right, because the ball goes past the non-stick side of the opponent who started to tackle.

The ball can be advanced in the alley with the least interference and, therefore, with greater speed. Between the defending end line and the attacking 25-yard line, player should pass the ball to one of her wings as quickly as possible. Place the ball ahead so that the wing can pick it up while running at full speed. When making a pass to a wing, aim for the corner of the field. This will prevent the ball from going out over the side line, no matter how long the pass might be or how far the wing must go to catch up with it.

A wing who has the ball should dribble down the field at full speed and should keep out in the alley in order to spread the defense and not crowd her own forwards. If the opposing halfback approaches to tackle, the wing can either dodge or pass. If she outruns her defense she should go straight towards the goal and shoot as soon as possible, passing only if tackled. As she approaches the 25-yard line, she should prepare to pass the ball in order to move it into scoring position. Whenever possible, the ball should be centered about the 25-yard line, before the defense players move back into position. Look before a pass and choose an opening. The pass depends on the positions of the other players. If the opposing defense is covering deep (see page 76), use a flat pass to the inner or center. If the opposing defense is marking (see page 73), use a hard pass ahead that will go in back of the defense permitting a forward to rush in to pick it up. After passing the ball, stay near the edge of the striking circle ready for an opening to shoot and prepared for any clearing shots from the defense.

A wing taking a corner hit (see page 109), should know definitely to whom she is going to pass. The drive must be strong and accurate.

The speed and placement of the pass will depend on the preferences of the player to whom she is hitting.

A defense player should initiate the attack as soon as she gains possession of the ball. Out in the field she should make a clearing shot to a free player or through an opening. The pass should be made to allow the forward to pick it up while running at full speed towards the goal. If there is no player free, or no opening visible, dribble at full speed in order to draw off an opponent or move into a better position. If an opponent is very close and blocking all the openings, use a dodge.

When the ball is near or in the striking circle, clear the ball, hard and forcefully, away from the goal or to the nearest side into an opening. When in dangerous territory, never make a clearing shot across the goal.

In making a pass, keep in mind that every pass should initiate an attack. It should go directly to an unmarked team player into an opening (see page 73), or through a space in back of the defense. Merely hitting the ball in the general direction of a team player is not enough and may be a wasted pass. Pass the ball to a team player at a point at which she may easily pick it up without checking her speed, turning, or waiting.

The correct timing of passes is very important. When to make a pass is something that cannot be coached. It is instinctive, and the result of experience. The pass must be executed at the moment there is a space or an opening—before an opponent is close enough to tackle or block its passage but delayed just long enough to draw the opponent away from the receiver or the opening.

How hard the ball should be hit on a pass depends on how far away the receiver is, how close the opponents are, how much time there is to execute the pass, and how fast the receiver of the pass is moving. Make it as easy as possible for a team player to pick up the pass, keeping in mind that the opponent will try to gain possession of the ball first.

Before learning to pass effectively, a player must have not only the technical skills to control the ball and to hit it to the exact spot desired, but also good judgment. Thought and planning are necessary for deciding, in each instance, where and how to pass. The direction, speed, and timing of the passes depend on the positions of all players, and varying situations make it impossible to establish definite rules as to the correct place and time for passing.

FIG. 57. When to make a pass is something that cannot be coached. It is instinctive and the result of experience. The pass must be executed at the moment there is a space or an opening.

FIG. 58. Looking up before passing.

FIG. 59. Getting ready to pass.

Pointers for Passing:

A GOOD PLAYER:

DOES NOT	BUT ⟶ DOES
1. Pass too soon or too late, making an ineffective pass.	1. Have a definite reason for her pass, varying her stroke accordingly.
2. Forget to look up before passing to note the positions of her opponents and team players in relation to herself.	2. Know when to pass so that the receiver or space is used to the best advantage, and interception by her opponents is reduced to a minimum.
3. Pass the ball in such a way that the receiver is unable to pick it up in her stride.	3. Have the technical skill and ball control for accurate passing.

SHOOTING

A player who has the ability to shoot and score goals possesses intelligence, aggressiveness, determination, the ability to start quickly, and a speedy, strong, accurate drive, push, or flick. The following suggestions are addressed to one who would be an aggressive attack player.

Just before reaching the striking circle, 1) observe the goal area and the positions of the opposing defense and the goalkeeper, and look for an opening; 2) determine the angle of the shot to avoid having to look again when in control of the ball; and, 3) increase speed when approaching the striking circle.

On reaching the edge of the striking circle, 1) while dribbling, accurately aim for the unprotected spot of the goal, which is usually one of the corners; 2) shoot quickly and hard on the run, off either foot, at the first opportunity; and 3) rush the shot at goal with stick down. The ball may rebound off the goalkeeper's pads or the goalposts in the direction from which it came. If the attacking player is quick enough, there is another chance of shooting the ball into the goal cage before the defense can clear the ball. Many goals can be scored on the rebound from a goalkeeper's pads. Rushing the shot at a goal may tend to upset the goalkeeper and make her clear the ball hurriedly without time to choose her direction.

Other inside forwards must rush forward the instant the ball has been hit, in order to take advantage of other opportunities that will arise. They must be ready to cut for the ball if it is about to be intercepted. (See page 69.)

In general, the forward who drives from the edge of the circle follows her own shot. One forward rushes the goal to support her, while the other three forwards stay back toward the edge of the striking circle to wait for the balls that are cleared. Usually, the left inner rushes every drive for a goal because she is on the non-stick side of her forward line. Wings generally stay out near the edge of the striking circle. If a wing gets in a position to shoot for goal, she should rush her own shot; and the nearer inner should temporarily assume the wing's duties near the edge of the striking circle.

Those who have rushed, without scoring a goal, must get back quickly before another shot has been made by a team player, otherwise they may be offside. Forwards must move constantly to position themselves so that their feet and stick face in the proper direction to receive the ball.

As a player enters the striking circle she may find that there are several defense players between herself and the goal, or that the angle of the hit may be too acute, making it necessary to pass to another player.

From a spot near the goal, she must use a quick, wrist shot, such as a push or a flick. All the inside forwards should close in quickly, with sticks on the ground, to allow the goalkeeper very little opportunity to clear effectively. If the inside forwards find it impossible to break through due to the intelligent play of the defense players, and the circle is heavily guarded, a flat pass to either wing may open up an opportunity for a clear shot from the edge of the circle.

FIG. 60. Rushing the shot at the goal.

FIG. 61. Ball in the air as a result of a flick at the goal.

Pointers for Shooting:

A GOOD PLAYER:

DOES NOT	BUT ⟶ DOES
1. Evade the responsibility of scoring goals or let a team player put the ball in the goal.	1. Want to score goals.
2. Slacken her speed as she reaches the striking circle.	2. Increase her speed and take aim just before reaching the striking circle.
3. Give the ball an extra tap inside the striking circle before making up her mind to shoot.	3. Shoot at the goal as soon as the ball enters the striking circle, preventing her opponent from gaining time in which to recover and tackle.
4. Wait to place her feet in the most comfortable position.	4. Shoot for goal off either foot.
5. Quit, until the ball is in the goal.	5. Shoot for goal and follow up her shot.

RECEIVING PASSES

A player must practice receiving passes that come at varying angles and speeds and from all directions. There are no hard and fast rules in regard to the proper position to receive a pass.

Receiving passes well depends upon the technique of fielding the ball and body position. A player must have the ability to estimate the speed of an approaching ball, must consider her own progress and the time necessary to execute the stroke, and must be able to get the blade or face of the stick behind the path that the ball is taking. Then, these must be correlated so that the actual impact between the stick and the ball occurs at the precise moment when it is at the ideal spot for the particular stroke to be used.

In estimating the timing for any stroke, the player finds that the faster the speed of the ball, the quicker she must react, to be effective. When estimating the speed of the ball, she must take into consideration its direction. A ball traveling away from her requires an earlier backswing than a ball going in the same direction.

If the ball is approaching from behind on the right side, the feet should be pointing in the direction of the goal being attacked. Turn head and shoulders to the right to keep the eyes on the passer. Keep stick down and close to the ground, with the flat side of the stick in a position ready to receive the ball. If not already running, start to run or cut toward the ball the instant it is hit by the passer.

If the pass is coming either from behind or from the side on the left, turn head and shoulders to the left to watch the passer. Upon receiving the ball, keep feet pointing in the direction of intended motion. Keep the stick close to the ground, with the blade of the stick facing the direction from which the ball is coming and the body out of the way of the oncoming ball. If the pass is well-directed and coming at sufficient speed, and the ball is coming on the left side, let the ball cross in front before fielding it. When the ball is coming on the right side, turn the blade of the stick toward the ball on the right side and close to the near foot. This insures better ball control. Pick up the ball as soon as possible to proceed with it. Go to meet the ball; do not stand and wait for it to arrive.

When on the attack in the opponent's half of the field, it is necessary to keep on line with or slightly behind the forward who has the ball. This position affords a better opportunity to run forward or cut to pick up the pass and to continue. If a player places herself ahead of the ball, she will invariably have to stop the progress of the ball before continuing the attack. There is also the possibility of getting "offside." This is inefficient play.

Passes should be fielded while running at top speed and the ball so controlled that it can be passed or shot at a goal instantly. The blade of the stick should "give" as the ball makes contact with it. The ball must never be fielded close to the feet; a good reach in front or to either side of the body should be used.

FIG. 62. Position for receiving a ball approaching from in back and on the right.

Pointers for Receiving Passes:

A GOOD RECEIVER:

DOES NOT	BUT ———▶ DOES
1. Stand with her back to the goal she is attacking.	1. Keep her feet pointing in the direction the pass is to be taken, turning her head and shoulders to watch the passer.
2. Stand and wait for the ball to arrive, or stop the ball too soon.	2. Anticipate the direction of the ball and time her movements accordingly.

TACKLING BACK

A defense player who goes in to tackle and is passed, or a forward who has the ball taken away from her, must quickly turn around and try to retrieve the ball before her opponent has progressed too far. She must reverse her direction and gather speed without loss of time.

It is important for a forward to help her own defense by tackling back without interfering with the defensive play. If she is unable to retrieve the ball, she must try to spoil her opponent's pass or force her opponent to pass. By so doing, she will give her own halfbacks a better opportunity to get into position for interception. (See page 69.)

When tackling back, a player uses a left-hand lunge if the opponent is on the tackler's left. The circular tackle is used when the opponent is on the tackler's right. In tackling back on the right wing, the tackler should use the circular tackle, as she would be in the proper position to keep the ball from getting in toward the center of the field. A left-hand lunge, in the above instance, would not be advisable because, if the tackle is unsuccessful, the right wing is allowed to go on toward the goal or to pass the ball unchallenged. No opponent is between the right wing and the goal.

FIG. 63. Trying to catch the opponent.

Fig. 64. Right halfback tackling back.

When a tackler back is not able to do a good left-hand lunge or circular tackle, she will have to try a reverse stick tackle or a jab, which are spoil strokes used to put the ball out of control of the opponent.

Pointers for Tackling Back:

A GOOD PLAYER:

DOES NOT	BUT ⟶ DOES
1. Let another player do the tackling if she loses the ball.	1. Turn and tackle back immediately when she loses the ball.
2. Interfere with her own team player.	2. Wait behind or beside her team player if two players on opposing teams are struggling to gain possession of the ball.

INTERCEPTING

To intercept means to gain possession of the ball as it is being passed from one opponent to another. Knowing how to get the ball before the opponent does requires concentration and anticipation. No detailed plan can be made in advance, because everything depends upon the positions of the players and the position of the ball at the moment; and these positions cannot be predicted accurately.

In order to intercept, think and concentrate every minute of the game and continually watch the changing formation of the players.

Closely observe the position of the ball in relation to the players. Watch the blade of the opponent's stick to learn the angle of her pass. Focus attention on where she is looking, how she is turned, and what she has done previously. These are indications of her next move and will show where she is going to send her pass. Next, anticipate the direction of the ball, the direction to move, and the opponent's next move. At the last minute, run to the spot at which you think the pass will come, and move into position so that the ball can be played on the stick side. Play the ball at once.

Fig. 65. Anticipating the play. The player in the lighter tunic is getting ready to intercept so that she will get the ball before it reaches her opponent. Note that her stick is down near the ground.

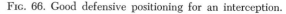

Fig. 66. Good defensive positioning for an interception.

Pointers for Intercepting:

A GOOD PLAYER:

DOES NOT	BUT ⟶ DOES
1. Stand and wait for the ball to come to her.	1. Run at full speed to meet the ball.
2. Lack finesse.	2. Anticipate.

BACKING UP

Backing up is a concern for defense players. To back up means to support and to play closely behind a team player who has the ball.

The halfbacks back up their forward line when their team is attacking. The reason for this is that, in case an attacking player loses the ball and the opponents try to get the ball on their attack, the backing up halfbacks can intercept a pass that might come through or they can tackle the opponent with the ball in order to get it back to their own forwards and, therefore, keep the opponents from getting on a sustained attack. Unless the halfbacks back up their forward line, their team will not produce an effective or a sustained attack. The defense starts the attack by giving its forwards the ball.

When the ball is on the right side of the field, the right halfback takes a position behind and halfway between her right inner and right wing. The center halfback takes a position between her right inner and her left inner. The same shift is used when the ball is on the left side.

It is important that the left halfback, center halfback, and right halfback back up their attack at the edge of the striking circle. They are vital to an effective attack. They must keep moving about just behind the circle in order to place themselves in positions to prevent the opponents from getting the ball to their forwards. The left halfback must move from the left wing position as far in as the left inner normally plays. The center halfback moves from the normal left inner to right inner territory. The right halfback moves from the right inner area to the right wing's area. If the halfback intercepts the opponent's clearing shot, she should shoot for goal or pass to a team player.

Either the left or right fullback must also back up the attacking forwards. Often the fullback on the side of the field where the ball is being played assumes the position of another halfback and plays up and backs up her attacking forwards. For example, if the ball goes into the attacking area on the left side, near the left wing or the left inner, the left fullback can back up the attacking movement. If the ball goes into the attacking area by the right inner or right wing, the right full-back backs up the attack. The distance she goes down the field depends on how quickly she is able to get back in a defensive position when her team loses possession of the ball. When the ball goes into the attacking area by the center forward, either fullback may back up. The fullbacks make this decision. Usually the fullback with the most stamina should be the one to do the most work.

The other fullback plays deep—in the center in her defensive half of the field, between the edge of the striking circle and the 25-yard line. There is no set rule on just where the fullbacks should play. They must be able to back up their attack and keep their opponents from scoring. As the play shifts from one side of the field to the other, the formation of the defense must change.

A defense player who is backing up a bully (see page 86) must be ready to tackle or intercept immediately if her opponent gains possession of the ball. The defense player must be ready to clear the ball away from the center if she gets the ball following the bully.

Fig. 67. Halfbacks back up the forward line when their forwards carry the ball toward the opponent's goal.

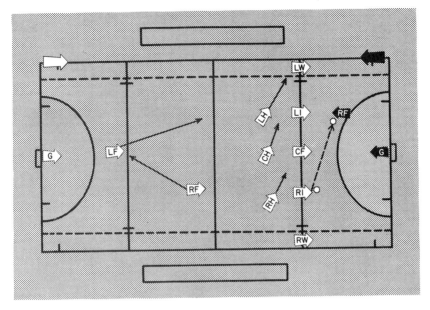

Fig. 68. The white team is on the attack. The ball is on the right; the right inner hits the ball to the left side of the field. Arrows show shift of defense when ball moves from right to left.

Pointers for Backing Up:

A GOOD PLAYER:

DOES NOT	BUT ⟶ DOES
1. Leave a large space between herself and her forward line when her forwards carry the ball toward the opponent's goal.	1. Play closely behind her forward line, ready to pick up the ball (if a team player loses it) and to return it to her or another member of the team.
2. Interfere with her other team players, even though she feels that she could accomplish the play with greater speed or skill.	2. Help out in an emergency, back up, and stand ready to assist.

MARKING

To mark is to guard the opponent closely enough to prevent her from receiving the ball and thereby to gain an opportunity to intercept the pass, or if the opponent gets the ball, to be in a position to tackle immediately.

Each defense player on a team is responsible for marking an opposing forward. The left halfback marks the opposing right wing, the

73

center halfback marks the opposing center forward, the right halfback marks the opposing left wing, the left fullback marks the opposing right inner, and the right fullback marks the opposing left inner.

Marking is important to good defense play. Forward line players mark on free hits (see page 115) and roll-in plays. (See page 97.) When marking, a player should try to gain a position enabling her to get the ball before her opponent does. She must not only mark her opponent but must be ready to intercept the ball if it should be passed into a space ahead. She must face her opponent and watch the player with the ball. This requires constant shifting of position in relation to the ball.

Fig. 69. Good marking of center forward by center halfback. Note: The center halfback is facing properly with her stick down, close to the ground.

On corner hits (see page 109), each defense player must come out quickly to mark her attacker. In the striking circle, each defense player must mark closely. Take position close to the opposing forward to prevent opponent from gaining a free shot at goal.

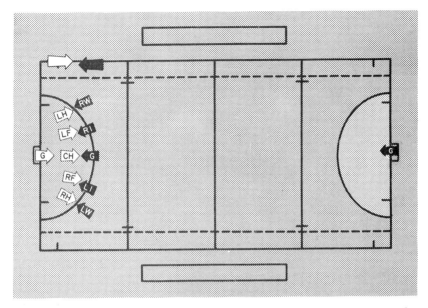

FIG. 70. Marking by defense in the circle.

FIG. 71. The halfback and fullback are marking their opposing forwards.

Pointers for Marking:

A GOOD PLAYER:

DOES NOT	BUT ⟶ DOES
1. Allow her opponent to be too far away from her.	1. Place herself close to her opponent on the ball side.
2. Get on the wrong side of her opponent.	2. Position herself so that she can get the ball before her opponent does.

COVERING

To cover means to attain a position from which to intercept any long, through pass, or to be ready to tackle any opponent who breaks through the other defense players on the team. Give team players a chance to get back in good defensive position before making the tackling move. Play back far enough so that no one may pass the ball behind you. The fullbacks and wing halfbacks must be prepared to go over to another forward when a halfback or fullback has been passed by her opposing forward.

FIG. 72. Covering formation of defense (white team) when opposing team (black) is in possession of the ball and on the attack, but not in or close to the circle.

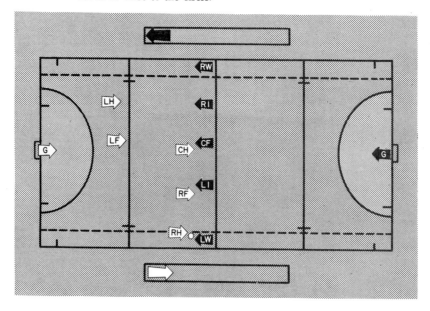

Figure Number 72 illustrates good covering formation of the defense when the ball is on the left side of the field. The black left wing has the ball. The opposing right halfback and right fullback mark. The center halfback marks her opposing center forward. The left fullback covers well back in the center of the field. In this position, she is prepared to, 1) intercept a long, through centering pass, 2) take the left inner in case the right fullback is passed, or, 3) get back to her right inner if the ball should go across the field. The left halfback also covers. She is ready to take the right inner if the left fullback is forced to go to the left inner. The right wing, in this situation, is left unmarked. She is not dangerous at the moment because she is so far away from the ball.

If the left inner had the ball, the right fullback would move in to tackle. Figure Number 73 illustrates the positioning of players when the white right fullback is about to tackle her opposing black left inner. The white right halfback marks her opposing left wing. The white center halfback marks her opposing center forward. The white left fullback moves in to cover her opposing right inner. The white forwards are alert and ready to receive a pass. The black halfbacks are backing up their forward line. The black fullbacks are covering.

Fig. 73. White right fullback about to tackle the opposing black left inner.

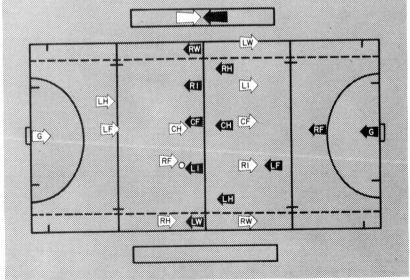

If the ball were on the right side of the field, the left halfback and left fullback would mark, and the right halfback and right fullback would cover. The center halfback marks her opposing center forward.

Figure Number 74 illustrates good positioning of the attack and defense when the ball is between two inners in midfield, on the far side of the field. All the forward line players face the direction in which they are going. The defense for both teams is positioned to meet the present situation and the probable ensuing one. The fullbacks nearest the ball back up their own team players and at the same time mark. The other defense players on both teams back up their forward line, mark the opposing forwards, or cover.

FIG. 74. Good positioning of attack and defense in midfield.

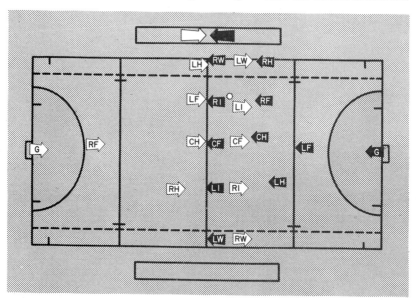

Figure Number 75 illustrates good positioning of the attack and defense in the striking circle. Note the good positioning of the backing up white halfbacks, the covering white fullbacks, and the good marking by the black defense. The white fullbacks are in covering position to intercept any clearing shot by the black defense. The black forwards are ready to receive a clearing pass.

Following are photographs and examples of play when a halfback or fullback has been passed by her opposing forward.

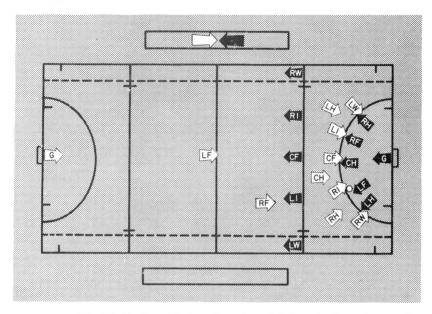

Fɪɢ. 75. Good positioning of attack and defense in the striking circle. The white right inner has the ball.

Fɪɢ. 76. Good marking and covering by the defense in the circle.

Fᴵɢ. 77. Good positioning of attack and defense when the ball is in the center of the field.

Fᴵɢ. 78. Defense play when the right fullback of the defending team is left behind, and the attacking left inner approaches the striking circle.

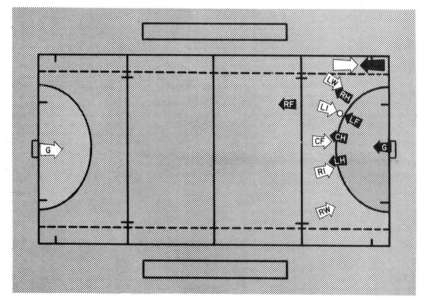

(1) Figure Number 78 illustrates the defense play when the defending right fullback has been passed by her opposing forward. The left inner has passed the right fullback. The right halfback con-

tinues to mark her own player. The right halfback does not move in to tackle the left inner who is free. This would leave her opposing wing unmarked and free to receive a pass. In order to prevent the left inner's reaching the scoring area unimpeded, the left fullback leaves her covering position and goes over to tackle the left inner. The center halfback marks on the ball side of her opposing center forward. The covering left halfback moves in to take the place of the left fullback to mark the right inner, leaving the right wing free. However, she is not dangerous at this moment. The right fullback must get back as quickly as possible to a covering position behind her own defense and in front of the goal, ready to make herself useful.

(2) If the left fullback were passed by the attacking right inner, the same principle would be used for shifting by the defense. If there are four or five defense players marking or covering, the halfback or fullback should tackle immediately.

(3) Let us suppose that the left inner passes the right fullback and also the left fullback, leaving the three halfbacks to take care of the five forwards. If the left halfback were to cross over to take the attacking left inner, the right side of the field would be left unguarded. In this particular situation, the right halfback should run back and cut in to be in position to meet the left inner or the left wing on the edge of the circle.

Whenever the defense is reduced to three or two players, a delaying game must be played. The defense must save their strength for the most crucial time. A defense player must wait and tackle the attacker as she gets close to the edge of the striking circle. In the interim, the defense hopes that the passed players can recover their own positions in time to help defend the goal.

(4) If a center forward passing her center halfback leaves the center halfback behind, as in Figure Number 79, the fullback, who is in the best position at the moment, must go in to tackle the opposing center forward who is free. The wing halfback moves in to take the inner who is left unmarked by the fullback when the fullback moves over to tackle the center forward. If the center forward passes the fullback who has come in to tackle, the other fullback must then move over to the center. Her wing halfback must also move in to take the unmarked inner. In this situation, the wings are free. However, it is more important to take care of the inners because they are more dangerous.

(5) When the right wing comes down the field with the ball, the left halfback must tackle if possible. The left fullback and center halfback mark. The right fullback and right halfback cover.

Fig. 79. Center halfback has been passed and is unable to recover. Right fullback is in position to take her team player's attacker (center forward). Left fullback is getting into a covering position.

Figure Number 80 shows that the left halfback missed the tackle and is left behind. The left halfback is unable to tackle back before the opposing right wing reaches the edge of the striking circle. The left fullback marks her right inner. The center halfback continues to mark her center forward. The covering right fullback moves over to take the attacking right wing. The right halfback leaves her opposing left wing and moves over to mark the left inner.

Fig. 80. Good positioning of defense if left halfback is left behind.

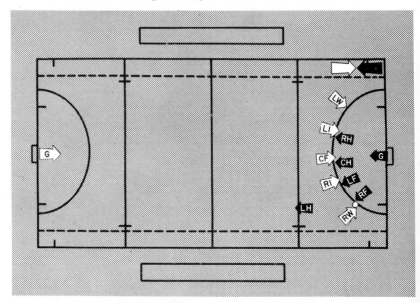

(6) If the defending right halfback were passed by the attacking left inner somewhere in midfield, the right fullback would not go out to the wing unless the ball were out of control and she knew definitely that she could get to it first. If the left wing had the ball well under control, the right fullback would not go until certain that the left fullback was in a good covering position. The center halfback marks her center forward, and the left halfback covers, opposite the right inner.

(7) If the left wing passes the opposing right halfback and the opposing right fullback, the three remaining defense players must stay in position to intercept. If the left fullback were to go across to the left inner, the entire right side of the forward line would be left unmarked, and a hard drive across the field would leave the path to the goal open. Insofar as scoring is concerned, the left wing is not dangerous as long as she stays out in the alley with the ball. If the wing cuts in toward the striking circle, she must be tackled either by the left halfback or by the left fullback.

Pointers for Covering:

A Good Defense Player:

DOES NOT	BUT ⟶ DOES
1. Concentrate on marking only her own opponent.	1. Place herself sufficiently far from her opponent to be able to intercept any through or diagonal passes made by an opponent; and tackle if an opponent breaks away or comes down the field alone with the ball; and tackle if one of her own team players has been passed.
2. Fail to learn by experience the best moves.	2. Understand the theory of covering.

INTERCHANGING

Interchanging is the actual exchanging of positions by two players of the same team. Interchange must be definite, clearly understood by the players involved, and done quickly. When the interchange is completed, the players should remain in their assumed positions until the play has changed to another part of the field, their team has gone successfully on the attack, or a goal has been scored.

There are times during a game when a forward line player might interchange, 1) when she has to go out of place to get the ball in order to pick up a pass, 2) when she is unable to get back on line with her team players after tackling back, or, 3) when she dribbles into another forward line position.

Let us suppose that a pass is made from a wing to her inner in the attacking area. The inner anticipates that her opposing fullback will intercept the ball. Instead of waiting for the ball, the inner should immediately cut or run toward the alley to meet the ball. If she gets the ball, she should dribble down the alley in the wing position, as fast as possible. The wing should move immediately into the inner's position to complete the interchange.

A situation might arise when the attacking white center halfback tackles the black center forward near the striking circle. The black center forward immediately tackles back and deflects the ball from her opponent's stick. Her black center halfback gets the ball and dribbles ahead into her center forward's position. The black center forward temporarily assumes the center halfback position.

Another example might arise when a center forward, who is ahead of her inner, goes to the inner's place to field the ball. If this should happen, the inner should move over to the center forward's position to prevent confusion.

Pointers for Interchanging:

A GOOD PLAYER:

DOES NOT	BUT ——————▶ DOES
1. Leave her assumed position until it is safe to move back to her own place.	1. Remain in her assumed position until the play has changed to another part of the field.
2. Play out of position without an understanding with her team player.	2. Have the interchange of positions clearly understood with her team player.

4

This chapter is to show skills and strategy used for the bully, the roll-in, the corner, and the free hit which are necessary for successful performance.

Every player on the team should know how to bully and the rules that apply to it. All forwards should be proficient at it, because they will have to bully several times during a game. All defense players should learn how to bully, because any defense player may have to participate in a penalty bully at some time during her hockey career, and, therefore, should know and understand what to do under the circumstances. Goalkeepers should practice bullying with their goal pads on, because no time is allowed for them to take off their pads.

An important phase of halfback play is the roll-in. When skillfully used, it should be of considerable advantage to the team taking it. There are two types of roll-in, the long roll-in and the short roll-in. A

Action for Advantage:
Bully; Roll-In; Corner; Free Hit

long roll-in is a long, hard, and fast roll up the alley, close to the side line and parallel to it. A short roll-in, a short, quick roll of the ball, may be used in any direction to a team player taking the roll-in.

There are two varieties of corners—the corner often called the "long corner," and the penalty corner or "short corner."

A free hit is a decided advantage which can be well utilized, provided the player takes the free hit quickly and the hitter has the ability to find an opening.

The suggestions made in this chapter should be used only as ideas to be built upon.

BULLY

The bully is used to start a game. Among the various types of bullies that may be used during a game are the center bully, the 25-yard line bully, a wing bully, on-the-spot bully, and a penalty bully.

The center bully is the play used by two players from each team (center forwards) to start the game in the center of the 50-yard line. The game is restarted by a center bully after halftime and after a goal is made.

The game is restarted with a bully at the 25-yard line opposite the place where the ball went out over the end line under the following circumstances:

1. If an attacker who is within the striking circle sends the ball over the goal line outside the goal posts.
2. If an attacker who is outside the striking circle sends the ball over the goal line.
3. If a defender, who is beyond the 25-yard line, unintentionally, in the umpire's opinion, sends the ball over the goal line.

FIG. 81. Center bully.

FIG. 82. Ball going out over the end line not between the goal posts.

FIG. 83. Twenty-five-yard line bully.

Of the two 25-yard lines on the field, the one used for the 25-yard line bully is that nearest the end of the field where the ball went out of bounds.

The spot on the 25-yard line where the bully is to be taken is determined by the place where the ball went over the end line, namely, at a point opposite and nearest to where it crossed the end line.

For a wing bully, the game is restarted with a bully taken within a yard inside the sideline, at a point opposite the spot where the ball went out. The opposing wings take the bully. A wing bully is taken:

1. When an attacking player is the last one to touch the ball before it goes over the end line in the vicinity of the alley.
2. When the ball goes over the end line near the alley, or over the side line, off the sticks of two opponents.
3. If the ball is unintentionally sent over the goal line near the alley by the defending team when beyond the 25-yard line.

The on-the-spot bully is used to restart the game after the umpire temporarily suspends the game. The ball is placed on a spot designated by the umpire, when, in her opinion, the ball should be awarded to both teams. This bully occurs under the following conditions:

1. In case of injury to a player.
2. After a foul made simultaneously by players of opposing teams.
3. For illegal substitution by players on both teams at the same time.
4. In case a player is temporarily incapacitated (by, for instance, a broken stick), and no foul is involved.
5. Interference with the progress of the game, such as dogs or spectators being on the field.
6. If the ball becomes lodged in the pads of the goalkeeper or the wearing apparel of a player. If this should occur inside the striking circle, the bully must be taken not less than five yards from the goal line.

A penalty bully is awarded when a defense player wilfully breaks a rule in the striking circle or a defense player fouls within the striking circle when a goal would have been scored by the attack if the foul had not occurred.

The bully is taken by the defense player who fouled and by any player selected by the attacking team, on a spot five yards in front of the center of the goal line. All other players must remain beyond the nearer 25-yard line, and must not take any further part in the game until the penalty bully has been completed. The game is restarted on either the center or 25-yard line.

A penalty bully may have to be taken again. It may result in a goal or penalty goal, or it may result in no score, depending on the following circumstances:

1. The penalty bully is taken again:
   a. If any other player interferes.

b. If the players taking the bully should bully improperly, or should foul simultaneously.

c. If the ball goes off the sticks of both players taking the bully, over the goal line, and not between the goal posts.

d. If the defense player puts the ball over the goal line not between the goal posts.

2. The penalty bully results in a goal, and the game is restarted with a bully in the center of the field:

a. If the defense player fouls.

b. If either player hits the ball over the end line between the goal posts.

3. The penalty bully is over with no score made, and the game is restarted with a bully in the center of the nearer 25-yard line:

a. If the attacking player fouls.

b. If the attacking player puts the ball over the goal line not between the goal posts.

c. If the defense player gets the ball outside the striking circle.

For the bully, two players, one from each team, stand squarely, in a comfortable stance, feet slightly apart, facing the side lines and each other. The feet remain stationary until the bully is completed, with the third striking of sticks.

Grasp the stick firmly with the left hand at the top and right hand a few inches below. Bend forward from the waist so that the head is down with eyes directly over the ball. Weight should be forward on the balls of the feet, knees slightly bent, and hands in full control of the stick. The stick is extended out in front and on the ground, the flat side parallel to the center line, 25-yard line, or imaginary line. The imaginary line is unmarked, meaning that the forwards position themselves as for a center bully or a 25-yard line bully on line with a particular spot chosen by the umpire in whose half of the field the bully is to be taken. The ball is placed on either one of these three lines between the blades of the two sticks.

To start the bully, each of the two players raises her stick slightly off the ground, and, alternately, three times, strikes the ground on her side of the ball and then the flat face of her opponent's stick just over the top of the ball. ("Ground—sticks . . . ground—sticks . . . ground —sticks . . . BALL!") The ball is in play as soon as it has been hit by one of the two players taking part in the bully.

All players must be at least five yards away from the two players participating in the bully and on the same side of the line as the goal they are defending—that is, they must be nearer their own goal line than the ball.

The object of the bully is to gain possession of the ball as soon as the bully has been completed (after the third striking of sticks), and to set the players on the attack.

FIG. 84. The bully. The stance should be a position from which it is possible to move at top speed.

FIG. 85. Striking of sticks.

All forward line players should cross over the line as soon as the bully has been completed, heading toward the goal they are attacking, except on a penalty bully, in which all players except the two players taking the bully must remain nearer the 25-yard line. A forward who remains behind will not be in a position to receive the pass. She must be ready to run forward quickly and receive the pass on the run. If she is slow in starting to run to meet the ball, the opposing back will have a chance to intercept.

The defense players who are backing up the bully must be alert and ready to tackle or intercept, immediately, if the opposing team gets the ball, or to clear the ball away if their own forward should send it back.

The successful forward in the bully or her backing up back should try to send the ball ahead to a team player as soon as possible. The wings should be used often on plays following the bully.

FIG. 86. Forwards should stand well away from the players taking the bully and be ready to cut in for the ball if necessary. In so doing, they will draw their opposing defense away from the center, and make spaces through which the ball may be passed.

If the bully takes place on the opponent's 25-yard line, the play should be toward the goal in order to get the ball into the striking circle as quickly as possible before the backs can tackle or intercept. A goal can thus be scored.

If the bully takes place on the attacking team's own 25-yard line, they must initiate a strong attack in order to get the ball down the field away from their own goal as quickly as possible. All defense players must cover all angles for any passes that may come through. The right inner will try to pass to her right wing who will pick up the ball on the run and break away up the alley for a sprint. The opposing backs will be ready to intercept the pass, but for this particular play the ball can be sent to the non-stick side of the opposing left halfback which will make it more difficult for her to intercept. The right inner may use a square pass to her right wing who, in turn, will send a diagonal pass back. This triangular pass is very effective.

A bully is not just a matter of hitting the ground and the opponent's stick three times and then hoping to gain possession of the ball. What you are going to do *after the bully has been completed* requires keen, advance thought and planning.

If an attacking team is to gain possession of the ball, it is essential to have some definite plan to secure the ball from the bully. If players are aware of the various angles from which the ball will emerge from the bully, they can plan a more successful attack or a stronger defense.

There are many variations of the bully that can be worked out by the individual player. Some of the methods used to secure possession of the ball after the bully has been completed and the possible action which may result are:

(1) Pull the ball close and out of reach of the opponent's stick, moving the left foot backward as the pull is being made; remain facing opponent. Step diagonally forward onto the left foot and hit the ball diagonally to the left. Be careful not to obstruct in this play by allowing the ball to go between the feet or putting the right shoulder between the opponent and the ball.

(2) Pull the ball close and push it diagonally forward to the right. A good way to do this is to pull it a few inches toward oneself with one movement of the stick and at the same time move at least one foot very quickly. Then, without hesitating, push or hit the ball diagonally to the right, stepping into the stroke with the left foot.

(3) Reverse the stick and push the ball behind the opponent to the right. Take a step on the right foot, keeping shoulders square to the side line to avoid obstruction, and quickly hit the ball diagonally forward to the right. This is a good bully to use when the opposing defense has blocked the space in front of the forward on the right.

(4) Bring the stick down to play the ball. If the opponent brings her stick down at the same time in the same position, put weight behind the stick, exerting a pressure against the ball. Pull the ball up over the opponent's stick, dribble the ball, or quickly pass it to a forward.

(5) Quickly reverse the stick and hit the ball back to the halfback, who will immediately pass the ball to a team player on either side of the field, catching the defending team out of position. This requires a great deal of practice, and the halfback must be ready for it. It is dangerous to use this play in the defending area.

(6) Use a flick or push stroke, passing the ball to the right, between opponent's legs when she is in a wide stance. The object of this is to make a square pass to a team player.

(7) At the third crossing of sticks, leave the stick up so that the

opponent might hit the ball directly to the halfback. This is often used by beginners and is successful only when it is a complete surprise to the opponent as she plays the ball forward.

THE LINEUP OF PLAYERS
FOR THE CENTER BULLY

Forward Line

LW—Left Wing	Is close to the side line, out in the alley, left of her center forward.
LI—Left Inner (Left Inside Forward)	Is left of her center forward and closer to her than the left wing.
CF—Center Forward (Center)	Stands directly in the center of the field.
RI—Right Inner (Right Inside Forward)	Is to the right of her center forward and closer to her than to the right wing.
RW—Right Wing	Is to the right of her center forward, out in the alley close to the sideline, and facing the field in a position to receive passes from the defense or her right inner.

Backfield Players

LH—Left Halfback (Left Half)	Is between her own left inner and left wing, about five yards in back of the center line.
CH—Center Halfback (Center Half)	Backs up her center forward, and is on the stick side of her opposing center forward.
RH—Right Halfback (Right Half)	Is in back of her right wing near the 5-yard line rather than in the alley. She plays on the ball side of her opposing left wing.
LF (LB)—Left Fullback (Left Back)	Covers deep in the center of the field in back of the center halfback near the 25-yard line. If the ball should go to the left side, she would move up immediately in order to mark the opposing right inner.
RF (RB)—Right Fullback (Right Back)	Is almost on line with, or a little diagonally behind her center halfback and on the stick side of the opposing left inner.
G—Goalkeeper (Goalie, Goaltender, Goaler)	Is about one yard in front of and in the middle of the goal cage.

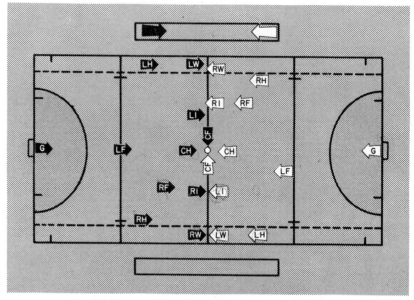

Fɪɢ. 87. Lineup of members of both teams. The black team is on one half of the field and the white team is on the other half, facing each other and in the direction they are going to attack.

THE LINEUP OF PLAYERS
FOR THE 25-YARD LINE BULLY

Attack Players (Black)

LW, LI, CF, & RW	Stand on the stick side of their opposing forwards.
RI	Bullies.
LH	Covers.
CH	Backs up her center forward.
RH	Backs up her right wing.
LF	Covers deep in the center of the field close to the center line.
RF	Backs up the bully.
G	Stands about a yard in front of and in the center of the goal cage.

Defense Players (White)

LW	Stands in the alley.
LI	Bullies.
CF	Moves over slightly toward her left inner, anticipating a short pass, and at the same time leaves an opening for a possible pass through.

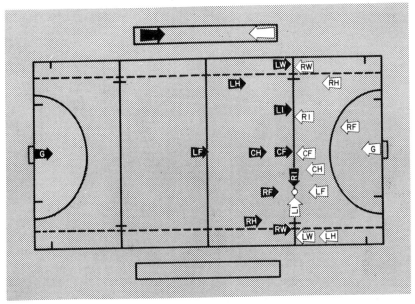

Fig. 88. Positioning of the attack and defense players for a 25-yard bully, taken by the inners.

RI	Moves closer to the center forward.
RW	Stands in the alley.
LH & CH	Back up their own forwards, and at the same time mark their opponents, ready to tackle or intercept any pass that might come through.
RH	Covers, and marks the black left inner.
LF	Backs up the bully.
RF	Covers.
G	Is alert and ready to change her position as soon as she determines the direction of the ball.

If the defense players on the white team desire a straight line defense, the right fullback should move up to the edge of the striking circle and the right halfback should move behind the right fullback and on line with the right inner.

Often a "V" formation is used, with the two nearer halfbacks slightly closer to the bully, and the fullback farther back.

THE LINEUP OF PLAYERS
FOR A PENALTY BULLY

All players, of both teams, must remain beyond the nearer 25-yard line.

95

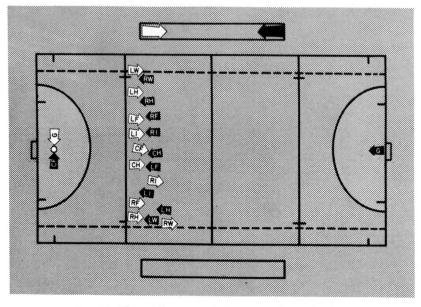

Fig. 89. The goalkeeper and the center forward taking the penalty bully.

CF (white attack) & G
(black defense)

Take the bully on a spot chosen by the umpire, which should be at least five yards in front of the center of the goal line.

Pointers for the Bully:

A GOOD PLAYER:

DOES NOT	BUT ⟶ DOES
1. Stand close to the players taking the bully.	1. Leave a wider space than legally allowed, to draw the opposing defense away from the center, and to open up spaces through which the ball may be passed.
2. Remain on the line, which would prevent her being in position to receive the ball.	2. Move as soon as the bully is complete.
3. Have a wide, unbalanced stance.	3. Get into a good, steady, balanced position over the ball.
4. Make wide, slow movements with her stick.	4. Have good control of her stick for fast movements.
5. Hit wildly at the ball at the completion of the bully.	5. Control her stick so that she can send the ball to her right inner, left inner, or her center halfback.

96

ROLL-IN

A roll-in is used when the ball is sent over the side line by one of the opposing team. When a player hits the ball out of bounds, the opponent who can get the ball the quickest to put it in play should take the roll-in. This player may be a wing, a halfback, or a fullback. Although anyone on the team may take the roll-in, in most instances the wing (side) halfbacks take the roll. However, the wing usually takes the roll-in when the play is in the vicinity of her opponent's goal in order to save time and also to avoid making the halfback play too far out of position, especially on the right side of the field where the space on her non-stick side will not be covered. The fullback may take a roll-in when the ball goes out over the side line near the center of the field but *only* if her side halfback and opposing forwards are not close by, or if the ball goes off far back in the defending area and her taking the roll-in will save time. If the fullback takes the roll-in quickly, she will catch her opponents off guard because they will not have had enough time to mark the attackers. The fullback may roll the ball in to her own halfback or inner.

Any player responsible for taking the roll-in should take it quickly so that the defenders will have less time to position themselves to mark the players or spaces or both. The player taking the roll-in must have both her feet and the stick outside the field of play. No player is permitted to stand inside the alley during a roll-in, and no player is allowed to stand outside the field of play, except the one taking the roll-in.

The player rolling the ball in faces in the direction of the attack, close to but outside the alley line, and she uses the hand nearest the side line to roll the ball. This means that wings, halfbacks, and fullbacks on the right side of the field must learn to roll the ball in with their left hands. Using the hand nearest the side line gives the player a chance to conceal the intended direction of the ball up to the last moment.

Hold the ball loosely in the fingers and palm of the hand, and hold the stick loosely in the other hand, resting the head of the stick on or close to the ground and keeping it out of the way and not in the field.

Swing the right arm straight back from the shoulder, parallel to the outside line and over the alley, so that the ball will go straight up the field close to the side line. A backswing must go directly back in the same straight line as that in which it will be delivered forward. The actual movement should be a smooth one, with the arm lifted well back and swung forward with rhythm and the fingers nearly touching the ground. A ball rolled in across the outside line will continue at that angle across the alley. If the hand is turned to direct the ball up the alley, the roll-in will lack the force that comes from the full use of an arm swing.

As the arm swings forward, step forward with the opposite foot, shifting body weight. The leg opposite the hand used must be in front, giving the arm complete freedom at the side of the body. Crouch low, bending the knees deeply with the back leg knee almost touching the ground. Do not kneel, as one must be ready to enter immediately into the play. Furthermore, a roll-in that is made from a kneeling position loses power and flexibility. Bring the hand forward close to the ground and release the ball as it reaches a point opposite the forward foot. The ball must touch the ground within one yard of the point at which it left the field. Do not spin or bounce the ball.

Follow through after the ball with the arm and hand. If it does not hit the ground within one yard after being released, or if it bounces, it is usually because the muscles are taut and the ball is held too tightly, making the release jerky and not at the right instant to be close enough to the ground. It is the coordinated swing of the whole body behind the ball and the amount of backswing that give force and distance to the roll.

The same preliminary motions are used for the short roll-in as for the long roll-in. The direction of the ball is changed at the last minute, according to the position of the hand when it is released. In order to roll the ball to the side or backwards, stop the forward swing of the arm when it is perpendicular to the ground, and change the direction of the swing before releasing the ball.

No matter how hard or where the player intends to send the ball, the body position and preliminary arm motion should always be the same. If they are not, the opponents will guess the intended direction, mark closely the possible receiver, and intercept the ball.

Roll-In Play Situations:

Roll-in situations must be considered from the viewpoint of both attack and defense. In the attacking area, the player who begins the play must be able to roll the ball forcefully, smoothly, and accurately. The roll-in must be taken quickly and must be varied in direction and speed; and sometimes it must be sent across to the center halfback and to the fullback. Every player of the attacking team, on the side of the field where the roll-in occurs, must be ready to receive it. The inner should stand away from the alley line to make a space or an opening for the roller-in. As the player taking the roll-in starts her swing for-

Fig. 90. Start of a roll-in.

Fig. 91. Follow-through
for a short roll-in.

Fig. 92. Follow-through
for a long roll-in.

ward, the inner should cut in toward the ball, timing her action to pick it up on the run. The fullback should be ready for a reverse-roll in the same manner.

Sometimes, in midfield, the two inners as well as the wings may go out to the five-yard line for the roll-in in order to vary the play. However, they should return to their usual places immediately afterwards. If a player stands where she expects to receive the ball, she makes it that much easier for her opponent. The roller-in must accurately aim for an opening or a spot where the receiver can run forward to pick up the ball. The wing should be close to the alley line and ready to dash up the field as soon as the ball leaves the hand of the halfback taking the roll, who must quickly choose the best opening and disguise her plans without disclosing the direction of the roll.

There are innumerable possible plays from various situations. Following are illustrations of some roll-in play situations resulting from the ball being hit over the side line. These should serve only as suggestions. Players are limited in their positioning, but all players have definite jobs to do and should be ready for any kind of a roll-in. The photographs show offense and defense positions from which to execute the play successfully or to block the play.

FIG. 93. Inner cutting in toward the ball as the player taking the roll-in starts her forward swing. Fullback is ready for a reverse roll.

RIGHT HALFBACK ROLL-IN
BETWEEN 25-YARD LINE AND CENTER LINE

Attack Players (White Team)

LW	Is ahead of her other forwards hoping a team player will get the ball and make a long drive to her side of the field.
LI & CF	Are on line with the right wing.
RI	Moves out close to the 5-yard line, in order to vary the play. She returns to her usual place afterwards.
RW	Moves diagonally ahead of her RH, who is taking the roll-in, and close to the 5-yard line.
LH	Covers.
CH	Backs up her forward line and is ready for any possible pass or roll-in.
RH	Has a choice of rolling the ball in to the RW, RI, CF, CH, or RF.
LF	Covers near the 25-yard line in the center of the field (not shown).
RF	Backs up her own team and is ready for a possible roll-in.
G	Is about a yard in front and slightly to the right of center of the goal cage.

FIG. 94. The black team hits the ball out over the side line off the field of play between the center line and the 25-yard line. This puts the black team on the defense and the white team on the attack. The white halfback takes the roll-in. (Illustration shows the white *right halfback* taking the roll-in.)

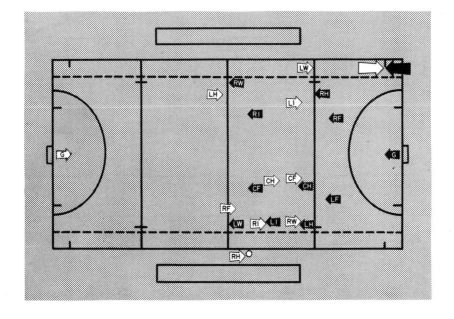

Defense Players (Black Team)

LW	Watches her RF, in case the roll is sent to her, and plays ahead of her other forwards hoping a member of her team will intercept the ball and send her a long, hard pass.
LI	Marks the opposing RI to allow the fullback to play her position.
CF	Marks her CH, places herself between the opposing CH and the opposing RH, and keeps her eyes open for a roll-in across the field.
RI	Stays on line with her CF.
RW	Plays ahead of her forward line, anticipating a long, diagonal pass from a teammate.
LH & CH	Mark their opposing forwards (RW and CF).
RH, LF, & RF	Cover and are in position to intercept any pass or tackle.
G	Is about a yard and slightly to the left of the goal cage.

RIGHT HALFBACK ROLL-IN
AT THE ATTACKING 25-YARD LINE

Attack Players (White Team)

LW, LI, & CF	Are on line with each other, slightly ahead of the ball.
RI	Does not move out close to the 5-yard line. Instead, she moves around and changes her position both to try to get the opposing LI away from the spot where she can mark, tackle, or intercept readily and to make a space for a roll-in.
RW	Is close to the 5-yard line, ready for a roll-in.
LH	Covers between the opposing C and RI, and is ready for a diagonal pass that might come through should the opponents secure the ball.
CH	Backs up her forward line and at the same time is ready to receive the ball from her RH.
RH	May roll the ball in to her RW, RI, CH, or RF.
LF	Covers toward the center of the field so she can move to her right or left quickly if necessary.
RF	Backs up her forwards (because the roll-in is taken on her side of the field), and is ready to receive the ball if sent to her.
G	Is about a yard in front of the goal toward the right side (not shown).

Defense Players (Black Team)

LW	Plays ahead ready for a hard pass from her team player in case her team controls the ball.
LI	Plays back, and tries to fill up a space that the opponent can't roll into.
CF	Loosely marks her opposing CH.
RI	Plays slightly diagonally ahead of the CF in a position of readiness, should her team control the ball.
RW	Moves out to the edge of the side line to draw her opposing left halfback, if possible. If her team does get the ball, she is then in a very strong attacking position.
LH & CH	Mark their opposing RW and CF.
RH	Temporarily leaves her opposing LW and moves back and in to cover.
LF	Marks the RI.
RF	Covers.
G	Stands slightly in front and to left center of the mouth of the goal cage.

FIG. 95. A black player hits the ball off the field of play at the 25-yard line. The ball goes to a white player for a roll-in, giving the white team the advantage of being on the attack. (Illustration shows the white *right halfback* taking the roll-in.)

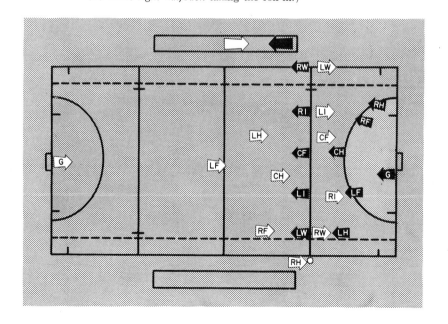

RIGHT WING ROLL-IN NEAR ATTACKING GOAL LINE

Attack Players (White Team)

LW, LI, & CF	Stay on line with the RW.
RI	Is on line with the RW and ready to cut for the ball when it is rolled in.
RW	Takes the roll-in.
LH	Covers between the opposing CF and RI.
CH	Marks her opposing CF.
RH	Marks the LW, and is ready to receive the roll-in.
LF	Covers.
RF	Watches her opposing LI and backs up the attack.
G	Plays about one yard in front of the goal cage.

Defense Players (Black Team)

LW	Marks the opposing RH.
LI	Moves back slightly and is ready to intercept the roll-in as well as to go on the attack.
CF	Stays ahead and out of the way of her own CF, ready to go if her team gains possession of the ball.
RI	Places herself on line with the CF, ready to go if her team gets the ball.
RW	Places herself in or close to the alley.
LH	Moves close to the 5-yard line and in such a position that she can mark the RW as soon as the RW has rolled the ball in.
CH	Marks on the ball side of her opposing CF.
RH	Marks the opposing LI.
LF	Marks the opposing RI.
RF	Covers between the LI and the CF.
G	Stands near the left goal post to block her non-stick side.

The following illustrations and descriptions are suggestions for possible plays for a roll-in which the person taking the roll-in might find useful.

(1) The right halfback, near her own 25-yard line, makes a long roll-in up the field, close to the side line, to be picked up by the right wing. The wing places herself outside the alley on the field of play and close to the roller-in, drawing her halfback with her. The closer to the side line the ball is rolled, the less chance there is for the opposing halfback to intercept it. The wing, already facing the direction of the intended path of the ball, runs down the alley after the speeding ball.

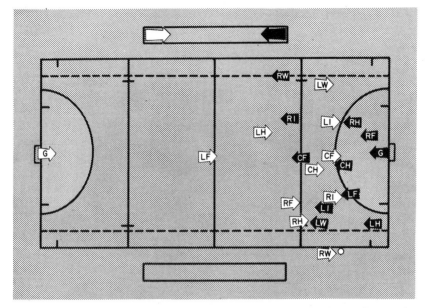

FIG. 96. A black attacking player hits the ball out of bounds near the end line, which gives the white team the ball, placing them on the attack. The white right wing takes the roll-in.

FIG. 97. Right halfback rolls down the field as close to the side line as possible.

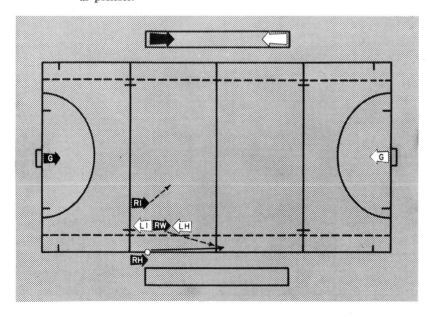

A left halfback will find it more difficult because she must intercept in the alley on her non-stick side. At such times she must place herself on the far side to reach more readily.

Note: The right wing has drawn her opposing left halfback, leaving space for a long roll up the alley.

(2) The left halfback, near her own 25-yard line, makes a short diagonal roll to the left inner, who runs diagonally forward to receive the ball in the middle of the alley and makes a long drive up the alley for the left wing. The left wing must dash across the alley and out to the sideline in order to pick up the pass on her stick side. To avoid wasting time, she must position herself before handling the ball.

Fig. 98. Left halfback rolls to left inner, who meets ball and drives it up alley to left wing.

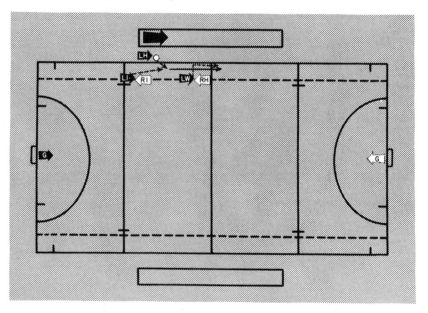

(3) Beyond the opponent's 25-yard line, the left wing makes a short roll into the alley. The left halfback goes to meet it and makes a long, hard drive through an opening toward the center of the field to the center halfback, or toward the striking circle behind the defense to her forwards.

Note: The left halfback must move in order to field the ball on her stick side so that she may pass quickly.

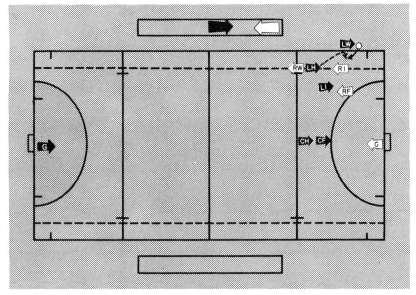

Fig. 99. Left wing roll-in to left halfback.

(4) Between the opponent's 25-yard line and the goal line, the right wing rolls the ball to the right inner between the opposing halfback and left inner. The right inner goes to meet the ball and makes a hard drive, behind the defense, into the striking circle, hoping the other forwards will rush in and shoot for goal.

Note: In this instance, the inner keeps her regular position.

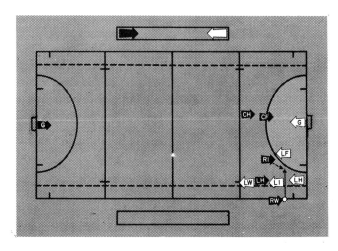

Fig. 100. Right wing roll-in to right inner.

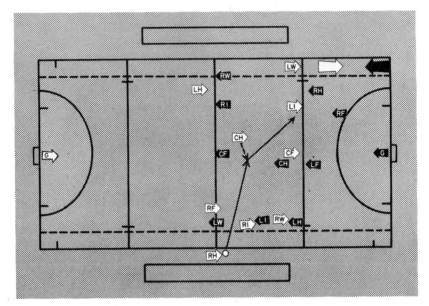

Fɪɢ. 101. Right halfback roll-in to her center halfback.

(5) The black team hits the ball out over the side line just beyond the center line in midfield. The right halfback on the white team rolls the ball on the diagonal across the field to her center halfback. The center halfback runs to meet the ball and immediately hits it ahead and across the field to her left inner.

This is a good play if the center halfback is not marked and if the right inner is not standing opposite the right halfback.

Pointers for Taking a Roll-In:

A Good Player Taking a Roll-in:

DOES NOT	BUT ⟶ DOES
1. Hold the ball tightly in the whole hand.	1. Grip the ball loosely with fingers outspread.
2. Use the roll-in only as a means of bringing the ball back into play.	2. Have a definite objective and use the roll-in to advantage for her team.
3. Bounce, loft, throw, or spin the ball onto the field of play.	3. Keep the hand with the ball close to the ground, to prevent the ball from bouncing or lofting.
4. Look at the spot where she is going to roll the ball in.	4. Have some deception.

5. Take her time getting the ball or getting to her position for the roll-in, as this would allow the defense too much time to get organized.

5. Take the roll-in quickly.

CORNER

A long corner is awarded to the attacking team when, 1) a defending team player touches the ball inside the striking circle and unintentionally sends it out over the goal line but not between the goal posts, 2) an attacker hits the ball outside the striking circle and then it is hit or glances off a defender into the goal, and, 3) the ball glances off the stick or person of the goalkeeper or off the stick of any other of the defending team behind the 25-yard line, over the goal line but not between the goal posts. The ball is placed not more than five yards from the corner of the field on the goal line or side line on that side of the field where the ball went out.

A penalty corner (short corner) is awarded to the attacking team to penalize the defense for intentionally hitting the ball over the end line. It is also awarded for any foul committed by a defense player within the striking circle. If the attack is about to shoot for a goal and is fouled, the umpire would hold her whistle and not stop the game to award a penalty corner, because this would not be advantageous to the attacking team. The penalty corner is for the purpose of giving the attack a better opportunity to score. When a penalty corner is awarded, the attacking player taking the hit may place the ball on the goal line not less than ten yards left or right of the nearer goal post. Whenever there is a choice, many teams prefer to have the right wing take the corner hit, because the forwards are in a better position to drive for the goal immediately, as they are driving on the non-stick side of the defense (opponents).

Corners and penalty corners are played similarly. The line-up of the attacking team depends on whether the hit is taken from the left or right of the goal. The attacking wing, on the side where the ball went out, hits the ball to any member of her team who must remain outside the striking circle until after the ball is hit.

The attacking player receiving the ball may not shoot for a goal until the ball has been controlled by being stopped, (not necessarily motionless), or has touched the stick or person of a defender. However, the ball must be stopped motionless if the hand is used. The attacking halfbacks place themselves behind their forwards so that they can field any balls missed by their own forwards, or cut off a pass intended for the defending forwards, or shoot if the opportunity presents itself. The attacking fullback, on the side of the field where the corner hit is taken, backs up her forwards; the other fullback, on the attacking team, covers deep in the center of the field near the center line and is ready to cover the entire backfield in a defensive capacity. Forwards rush the shot at the goal, and halfbacks back up and send the ball back into the circle if it should come out. Fullbacks are the last line of attack, and must stop the opposing forwards from reaching the ball.

Until the ball is hit, six of the defending players stand at least five yards away from the ball behind their own goal line, opposite and on the ball side of the attacking forwards for whom they are responsible. The other five members of the defending team must remain beyond the 25-yard line until the ball has been touched by a player other than the one taking the corner hit or until it has gone outside the striking circle.

In both kinds of corner, penalty corner and corner, the same general techniques may be used. The theory of attack and defense are the same. When the ball is hit hard and directly, the attacking players wait for it at the edge of the circle. When the ball is poorly hit or topped, the attacking players must go to meet it. The wing, taking the corner hit, must make a hard, accurate drive aimed at a point on the edge of the striking circle which can be easily played by her right inner, center forward, center halfback, or left inner. If the ball does not travel fast, it will be picked up by the outcoming defense. If the hit is not at a correct angle and cuts across the middle of the circle, it will be intercepted easily by the opposing team. A hard, well-placed hit will give the attacking players a little more time to shoot, and will make the defense players travel farther to get it. After the wing has made the hit, she must move into the striking circle and get herself on-side. If the ball is hit so hard that the receiving forward succeeds only in stopping its momentum, the other attacking forwards must be ready to drive for the goal the instant the ball is out of the receiver's control. Success depends upon accuracy, controlled fielding, and the quick, definite action of the individuals who take part in the play. Attacking halfbacks should be ready to receive, control, and pass or shoot for the goal any ball that might be missed by the forward or intercepted by the defense.

Generally speaking, the attacking player who is to receive the ball must be marked; that is, if the right wing is taking the corner hit, the right halfback, right fullback, and center halfback go out immediately to mark their opponent. The left fullback and left halfback move to a covering position. Defensive players should move as soon as the corner hit is taken. The goalkeeper should watch the forward who is about to receive the corner hit.

Figure Number 102 shows the two teams in position for a corner, which occurs because the defense (black team) last touched the ball before it went out of bounds over the goal line. The left wing of the white team is standing on the end line ready to hit the ball to her forwards who are around the edge of the striking circle. The black team defense players are lined up behind the goal line.

Figure Number 103 shows the left wing of the white team standing on the side line, ready to hit the ball to her forwards who are around the edge of the striking circle. The black team defense players are lined up behind the goal line.

THE LINEUP OF PLAYERS FOR A CORNER

Attack Players (White Team)

LW	Places the ball 5 yards from the corner. She drives the ball to a team player's stick, usually the LI or CF.
LI, CF, RI, & RW	Move slightly in the direction the ball is being hit, and stand well-spaced around the edge of the striking circle, ready to stop the ball immediately and drive for a goal. The CF moves on line with the goal post nearer to the ball.
LH, CH, & RH	Back up their forward line and cover the entire line from the corner hit to the opposite side line, ready to intercept, immediately, any clears that might be made by the defense.
LF	Covers close to the 25-yard line because she is nearer the corner hit.
RF	Covers deep toward the middle and center of the field, ready to cover the entire backfield in a defensive capacity.
G	Places herself in the center of the goal and about a yard in front.

Defense Players (Black Team)

LW, LI, CF, RI, & RW	Stay beyond the nearer 25-yard line until after the ball is played by another player or has gone out of the striking circle.
LH & CH	Stand in back of the goal line, opposite their opposing forwards (favoring the ball side) ready to run, as soon as the ball has been hit, to intercept or mark their opponents immediately.

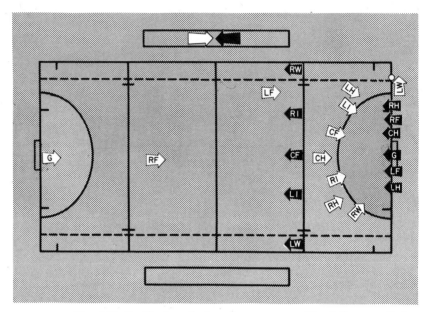

FIG. 102. Positioning of players on a corner. The ball goes off the stick of a black team player unintentionally over the goal line on the left side of the goal posts. The white left wing takes the corner hit.

FIG. 103. The wing takes the corner hit at the side line.

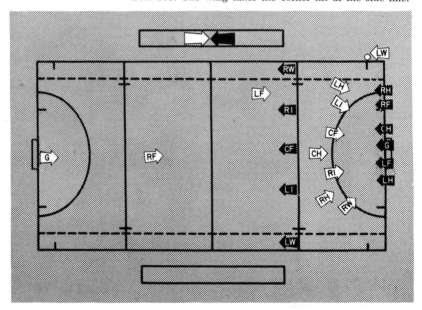

RH	Stands behind the goal line close to the edge of the circle, ready to intercept the hit or mark her opposing wing after the hit is taken.
LF & RF	Stand opposite their opposing forwards behind the goal line ready to run when the hit is taken.
G	Stands inside the mouth of the goal behind the end line.

THE LINEUP FOR A PENALTY CORNER

Attack Players (White Team)

LW, LI, CF, & RI	Stand at the edge of the striking circle ready to stop the ball immediately and drive for a goal.
RW	Places the ball ten yards away from the nearer goal post on the goal line. She drives the ball to one of her team players who is standing at the edge of the circle.
LH, CH, & RH	Back up their forwards.
LF	Covers between the center line and the 25-yard line in the center of the field.
RF	Covers close to the 25-yard line.
G	Stands in front of and in the center of the goal cage.

Defense Players (Black Team)

LW, LI, CF, RI, & RW	Remain beyond the 25-yard line until the ball either has been played by a player other than the player taking the hit or goes out of the circle.
LH	Places herself 5 yards from the RW toward the goal side, ready to intercept the pass and to mark the RW after she has hit the ball.
CH	Stands in back of the goal line opposite her opposing CF on the ball side, either inside the goal cage with the goalkeeper or outside. She is ready to dash out to mark the center forward the moment the ball is hit.
RH, LF, & RF	Stand in back of the goal line opposite their opposing forwards (LW, RI, and LI), and are ready to run out to mark their opponents and to intercept a pass the instant the ball is put into play.
G	Stands inside the mouth of the goal.

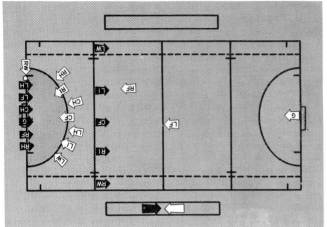

FIG. 104. A defense player (black) fouls inside the striking circle. The attacking team player (white) RW takes the corner hit.

FIG. 105. Eager opponents ready to go.

FIG. 106. A keen defense is all out at the correct moment.

Pointers for a Corner or a Penalty Corner:

A GOOD WING TAKING THE HIT:

DOES NOT	BUT ⟶ DOES
1. Hit the ball to the same inner continuously, as the other team will anticipate this and play her.	1. Let the wing on the other side take the corner hit to vary the play.
2. Hit the ball aimlessly.	2. Know to whom she is going to hit the ball and hit it hard and directly to her stick.

A GOOD ATTACKING FORWARD:

DOES NOT	BUT ⟶ DOES
1. Let the ball rebound too far forward.	1. Learn to stop the ball close to her stick and hit it quickly with a short backswing.
2. Aim at the goalkeeper.	2. Shoot for the corners of the goal.
3. Go after the ball on her left if it glances off her stick to her non-stick side (except the left wing).	3. Let the forward on her left side take any ball that glances off her stick to her non-stick side. She even moves away from the ball to give her team player a space to go through.
4. Use the non-stick dodge on a corner play as the ball is apt to go to a defense player who is very fast in coming out from the end line.	4. Learn to do a quick, closely controlled dodge. A little scoop over the defense's stick or a short pull of the ball toward herself may cause the defense player to overrun the ball leaving her in a free position for shooting.

A GOOD DEFENDING FORWARD:

DOES NOT	BUT ⟶ DOES
1. Wait just beyond the 25-yard line as though she were a spectator or without thinking or planning.	1. Remain alert while waiting just beyond the 25-yard line, in order to move purposefully the moment she can see when and where the ball is coming out.

FREE HIT

The free hit is awarded to one team if the other team fouls. Except when a player fouls in the circle, a free hit is taken on the spot where the foul occurred. Everyone must stay at least five yards away from the player taking the hit. A free hit is a decided advantage that can be well utilized, provided the player takes the free hit quickly and the hitter has the ability to find an opening.

When taking the free hit, a player may use the drive or push stroke. The ball must be motionless before striking, and may not be played again until another player has touched it. If a poor hit is made and the ball travels a few inches, place the stick just behind the ball, ready to take it away from the opponent as she tries to gain possession of it.

The nearest defense player on the team fouled against should run to the spot where the free hit is to be taken. If the ball is close by, she should pick it up and put it on the spot where the foul occurred; if the ball is not near, a team player should retrieve it to avoid wasting time.

While running to the spot to take the free hit or while waiting for the ball, the hitter should decide to whom and where she is going to direct her pass. The faster the free hit is taken, the greater the advantage. Players on the team should be alert and quick to get the ball and to position themselves. It is impossible for the opposing defense players to cover and mark closely at the same time; and if the free hit is taken quickly, the opposing forwards cannot get back fast enough to mark. If the hitter does not see either a space or a forward who is free for her pass, a little pass back to the side or to one of her defense will open up the play. This pass to her defense may confuse the opposing defense and give one of her own forwards a chance to get free.

Attacking forwards must position themselves to receive the ball. They should draw apart to make openings for a pass and be ready to run for the ball as soon as it has been hit. The hitter must be sure to hit the ball in such a way that the receiver can pick it up easily on the run.

If an attacking forward or halfback is awarded a free hit just outside the striking circle, the inners must move away from the center to draw the opposing defense away, thus leaving two or more openings through which the hitter may send a short, not-too-hard pass. The ball may go into the striking circle behind the opposing defense, or it may be a flat or direct pass to a team player who may cut for it. The forwards should dash for the ball and shoot immediately.

The defending team players must place themselves in a position to mark or cover. The defending forwards should mark the opposing forwards, so that their own defense players are free to mark or cover the space.

In the defending area, especially in or near the striking circle, free hits must be taken quickly and with long, hard drives through an opening, away from the goal but never across the goal. A free hit taken by the defense inside the striking circle should be taken by a fullback or a wing halfback in order to get the ball to the side and farther from the goal.

Following are illustrations of a defense player taking a free hit in different areas of the field. It should be remembered that there are many other possible variations which can be developed from these suggested plays.

RIGHT WING FREE HIT NEAR THE STRIKING CIRCLE

Attack Players (Black Team)

LW, LI, CF, & RI	Stay on line with the right wing who is taking the hit.
RW	Takes the free hit. She may pass the ball to her RH, RI, or CF through a space into the striking circle, permitting them to run and shoot for a goal.
LH, CH, & RH	Back up their own forwards.
LF	Covers.
RF	Helps to back up the attack.
G	Stands about a yard in front of the goal line in the center of the goal cage.

FIG. 107. A white player fouls near the striking circle. The black right wing takes the free hit to give her own halfback a chance to be in a better position.

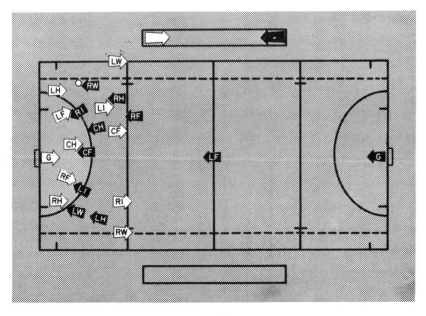

Defense Players (White Team)

LW	Moves near the 25-yard line, and near the outside edge of the field.
LI	Moves back to mark the opposing RH.
CF	Moves closer to her left inner, and keeps her eyes on the opposing CH.
RI & RW	Remain close to the 25-yard line.
LH	Waits to see who controls the play and is ready to take her opposing RW.
CH	Marks her opposing CF.
RH	Covers the space on the diagonal and marks her opposing LW.
LF	Marks her opposing RI.
RF	Marks her opposing LI.
G	Is close to the left goal post, blocking her non-stick side.

RIGHT HALFBACK FREE HIT NEAR THE 25-YARD LINE IN OPPONENT'S HALF OF THE FIELD

Attack Players (Black Team)

LW, LI, CF, RI, & RW	Are ahead of the player taking the hit.
LH & CH	Back up their own forward line.
RH	Takes the free hit. She may pass to her RI, CF, or CH.
LF	Covers.
RF	Backs up the attack.
G	Stands about a yard in front of the goal line in the center of the goal cage.

Defense Players (White Team)

LW	Is out near the side line on the 25-yard line.
LI	May move back in order to try to intercept the free hit.
CF	Marks her opposing CH.
RI & RW	Remain slightly ahead of their CF to wait for a clear.
LH & CH	Mark their opposing forwards.
RH	Keeps her eyes on her opposing LW.
LF & RF	Mark their opposing forwards.
G	Stands close to the left goal post blocking her non-stick side.

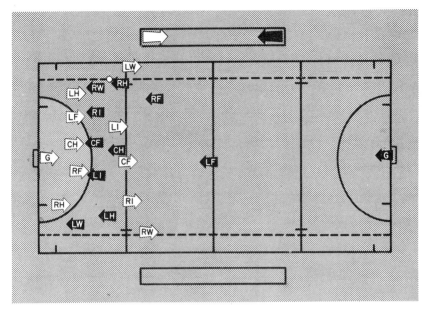

Fig. 108. A player on the white team fouls near the 25-yard line. The black halfback takes the free hit.

RIGHT HALFBACK FREE HIT BETWEEN THE TWO
25-YARD LINES IN THE OPPONENT'S HALF OF THE FIELD

Attack Players (Black Team)

LW, LI, CF, RI, & RW	Are on line with one another.
LH	Backs up.
CH	Backs up her CF.
RH	Takes the free hit. She may hit the ball to any one of her forwards, but it would be better to hit it to her RW or RI.
LF	Covers.
RF	Backs up.
G	Remains about a yard in front and in the center of the goal cage.

Defense Players (White Team)

LW	Places herself in the alley on line with her CF.
LI	Moves back and places herself between the opposing CH and RH in order to try to intercept the ball.
CF, RI, & RW	Stay ahead of their LI, ready for a pass.

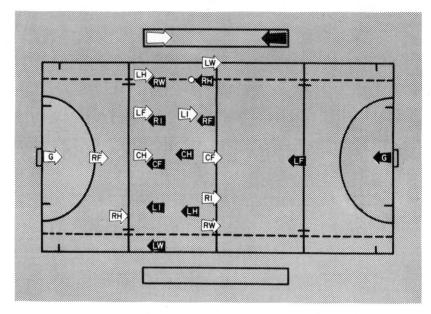

Fig. 109. A player on the white team fouls near the alley, between the two 25-yard lines in the opponent's half of the field. The black team RH takes the hit.

LH	Marks her opposing RW.
CH	Marks her opposing CF and tries to place herself between her opposing CF and RI.
RH	Covers.
LF	Marks her opposing RI.
RF	Covers.
G	Stands about a yard in front and in the center of the goal cage.

CENTER HALFBACK FREE HIT
BETWEEN OWN 25-YARD LINE AND CENTER LINE

Attack Players (Black Team)

LW, LI, CF, RI, & RW	Stay on line with one another and ahead of the ball.
LH	Backs up her forward line and is in position to receive the hit.
CH	Hits the ball to one of her forwards, her LH, or to a space in back of the opposing defense.
RH	Backs up her forward line, ready to move into a space if necessary.

LF	Covers deep in the center of the field in front of the striking circle.
RF	Covers and stands between the opposing LW and LI.
G	Stands about a yard in front of the goal line in the middle of the goal cage.

Defense Players (White Team)

LW	Is in the alley on line with her CF.
LI	Moves back to watch her opposing inner, ready to intercept the free hit.
CF	Moves ahead to wait for a pass which might be given to her if her own defense should intercept the hit.
RI	Moves back to watch her opposing LI, and is ready to help relay a pass to her wing if her team players should intercept the hit.
RW	Moves up on line with her CF, ready for a pass from her defense.
LH	Keeps her eyes on her opposing RW and RI.
CH	Marks her opposing CF. She places herself between her opposing CF and CH, hoping to intercept a pass which might be directed to either one.

FIG. 110. A player on the white team fouls as she approaches her opponent's 25-yard line. The black team CH takes the free hit.

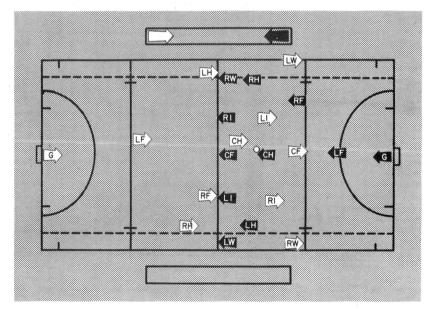

RH   Is between LW and LI, on about the 5-yard line, slightly in back of her RF.

LF   Covers in the center of the field in front of the striking circle, ready to move if the pass is directed to the RI or RW.

RF   Marks her opposing LI.

G   Stands about a yard in front of the goal line in the middle of the cage.

CENTER HALFBACK FREE HIT
NEAR THE EDGE OF THE OPPONENT'S STRIKING CIRCLE

Attack Players (Black Team)

LW   Plays outside the circle.

LI   Moves away from the center to draw her opposing RF out. She is positioned and ready for a drive at goal.

CF   Is ready and in position to dash for the ball and shoot for goal.

RI   Moves away from the center to draw her opposing LF out.

RW   Plays outside the circle.

LH   Backs up her forward line.

CH   Takes the hit. She may hit through an opening for one of the inners or the CF to play.

FIG. 111. A white-team player fouls in the center of the field near the striking circle. The black CH takes the free hit.

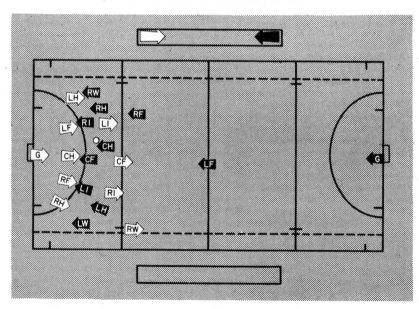

RH   Backs up her forward line.
LF   Covers.
RF   Backs up and covers.
G   Stands in the middle of the cage about a yard in front of the goal line.

Defense Players (White Team)

LW   Plays out in the alley near the 25-yard line.
LI   May move back to mark her opposing RH.
CF   Places herself near the 25-yard line.
RI   May move back to mark her opposing LH.
RW   Plays near the 25-yard line.
LH   Marks her opposing RW until she determines the direction of the ball for her next move.
CH   Marks her opposing CF.
RH   Marks her opposing LW until she determines the direction of the ball for her next move.
LF   Marks her opposing RI.
RF   Marks her opposing LI.
G   Stands in the center of the goal line about a yard in front of the cage.

RIGHT FULLBACK FREE HIT
NEAR THE GOAL LINE OUTSIDE THE STRIKING CIRCLE

Attack Players (Black Team)

LW, LI, CF, RI, & RW   Stay near the 25-yard line.
LH   Marks the opposing RI.
CH   Marks her opposing CF.
RH   Gets free in case her fullback wants to pass to her.
LF   Covers.
RF   Takes the free hit. She may drive the ball to her RH or RW.
G   Stands in the center of the goal cage and about a yard in front of the goal line.

Defense Players (White Team)

LW   Marks the opposing RW.
LI   Places herself between the opposing RH and RF, and tries to intercept the ball.
CF, RI, & RW   Stay on line with each other.
LH   Marks her opposing RW.
CH   Places herself between her opposing CF and CH, and tries to intercept the ball.

RH   Covers.
LF   Marks her opposing RI.
RF   Covers.
G   Stands in the center of the goal cage and about
                a yard in front of the goal line.

Fig. 112. A white-team player fouls near the goal line outside the
striking circle. The black RF takes the free hit.

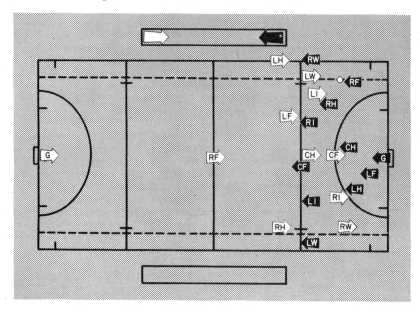

RIGHT FULLBACK FREE HIT
JUST OUTSIDE THE STRIKING CIRCLE

Attack Players (White Team)

LW   Stands near the side of the field, diagonally ahead of the
                ball, beyond the 25-yard line.
LI   Is slightly in back of the LW in her own area.
CF   Is in the middle of the field on line with her inner.
RI   Is diagonally back from the CF in her own area, ready
                to cut to receive the hit or to dart into a space to pick
                up the free hit.
RW   Is at the edge of the side line, ready to cut or pick up
                the ball if it is a through pass.
LH   Marks her opposing RI.

CH   Makes herself available to receive the free hit. She is not only ready to cut to help the player taking the hit, but is also ready to mark the opposing CF in the circle.

RH   Tries to place herself in order to relay a possible pass from her fullback, and is ready to cut to help out her team player taking the hit, or ready to mark her opposing wing if the opposite team controls the ball.

LF   Covers.

RF   Takes the hit. She may pass the ball to her RH or CH, or may make a through pass.

G   Stands about a yard in front and in the center of the goal cage.

Defense Players (Black Team)

LW   Is out near the side line ready to intercept any pass that may be directed for the RH or RW.

LI   Remains close to her opposing RH, ready to intercept any pass coming in that direction.

CF, RI, & RW   Stay on line with each other.

LH   Marks her opposing RW.

FIG. 113. A black player fouls just outside her opponent's striking circle on the left side of the field. The white right fullback takes the free hit.

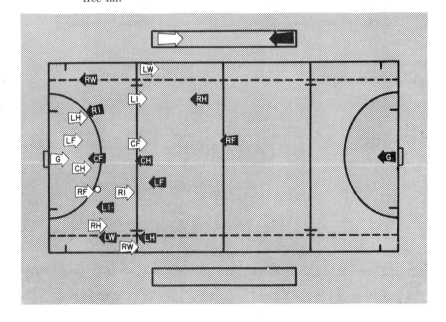

CH   Places herself between her opposing CF and RF in order to intercept the ball within that area.

RH   Covers.

LF   Marks her opposing RI and places herself in order to cover the space where the hit might possibly be directed.

RF   Covers deep toward the middle and center of the field.

G   Places herself about a yard in front of and in the center of the goal cage.

Pointers for Free Hits:

A GOOD PLAYER TAKING A FREE HIT:

DOES NOT	BUT ⟶ DOES
1. Pick up the ball and walk with it to the spot where the hit is to be taken.	1. Run with the ball to the spot where the hit is to be taken and take it quickly before all players and spaces are marked.
2. Hit the ball directly to an attacking forward if the opposing defense moves with the forward.	2. Look to see whether it is better to put the ball onto a player's stick or into a space ahead.

A GOOD PLAYER WAITING TO RECEIVE THE HIT:

DOES NOT	BUT ⟶ DOES
1. Place herself in such a position that both she and a space are marked by her opponent.	1. Create spaces by drawing her opponent aside to outwit her.

A GOOD DEFENSE PLAYER:

DOES NOT	BUT ⟶ DOES
1. Let the attack get the ball without opposition.	1. Try to "block" the opponent's free hit.

5

Each player of field hockey is most interested in her own team position; coaches are interested in all positions. New players try to determine which position on a team would be most interesting and suitable for them. Chapter 5 might be titled the "Who, When, Where and Why" for players in the varying situations which they will encounter in actual play at their specific positions. The design of the chapter, with questions and answers concerning each position given in the order of the team lineup, will enable all readers to find very readily the material they particularly need.

This Chapter will also serve as a ready-made test program for players and coaches who may wish, through self- or class-testing, to determine how much has been learned concerning the unique duties of the individual players.

Positions —
How Are They Played?

Wings

Wings must be fast, strong, and aggressive, and must have good stickwork.

1. *Question:* What is the most important work allotted to the wing?
   Answer: The wing must carry the ball down the field at full speed and either take it in to shoot or place her pass so that it eludes the defense and may be picked up by her other forwards or herself on the run.

2. *Question:* Where should the wing position herself?
   Answer: The wing should keep out in the alley in order to keep the game open; cut to receive a pass before the opposing halfback can intercept the ball or tackle; and dribble near the side line to draw out the opposing halfback, thereby leaving more space behind her in which to get passes through.

   Generally speaking, a wing should stay on line with her forward when in her opponent's half of the field, and should keep ahead of her forward when in her own half of the field.

FIG. 114. Considerable mobility of body movement is needed to master the technique of the center pass or a stinging shot at the goal.

3. *Question:* If the right wing stays out beyond the side line, how can she get the ball?

   Answer: She must run to meet the ball. This may mean running back toward her own goal. When she has fielded the ball, she will have to dribble it in a small circle, clockwise, around her opponent in order to get by her. She can do one of three things:

   a. Make a hard pass across to the center or other inner or wing;

   b. Make a triangular pass—pass the ball to her inner and then run at top speed back to the side line to receive the ball immediately. By this time her opponent should be behind her; or

   c. If her footwork and stickwork are good and the way is open, she should herself continue on with the ball and take it out. She must travel fast with it, as her opponent is behind her.

4. *Question:* If the wing stays out in the alley, can she ever take the ball into the striking circle and shoot for goal?

   Answer: Yes, but she must choose her moment. If she is free, she can cut in toward the edge of the circle. Her shot should be hard and accurate.

5. *Question:* Why is it poor play when a wing keeps the ball too long on the attack?

   Answer: A wing who keeps the ball too long on the attack gives the opposing defense time to position themselves—to cover and mark closely the other attacking forwards and reduce the openings for other forwards to score—or gives her opposing halfback a chance to tackle.

6. *Question:* How does the wing help her own attacking halfback?

   Answer: When her halfback has possession of the ball or is trying to get it, the wing should move into a space ahead of her halfback and well out near the side line, with her back to it, so that the halfback can find her easily. If the halfback is near the edge of the circle, the wing should move to one side, ready for a short pass or ready to move out of her way if she wants to have a shot at the goal.

   When the halfback is defending, the wing drops

back quickly beyond the 25-yard line, ready for a short pass from the halfback out of the circle and ready to mark the opposing wing.

7. *Question:* What is the responsibility of the wing when her own team is attacking in and around the striking circle?

Answer: A wing must be ready not only to shoot for a goal when the opportunity arises but also to retrieve a clear. She must be able to send the retrieved ball back to another forward or halfback who is free, to send the ball back with a pass behind the defense, or to make a quick shot or flick at the goal.

8. *Question:* Is it necessary for a wing to learn how to tackle?

Answer: Yes. Whenever the ball is taken away from her she should tackle back immediately. She should not let her opponent get away without opposition.

9. *Question:* When the opposing defense gains possession of the ball and starts moving down the field, what does the wing do?

Answer: The wing must run just as fast as her own halfback in order to be close enough to receive any pass her own defense player may want to give to her. She should never leave a large space between herself and her defense when the opposing forward has possession of the ball.

10. *Question:* How hard should the wing hit when she takes a corner hit?

Answer: As hard as she can. The harder she hits, the faster the ball will reach her forwards; and the faster her own team gets it, the less chance the defense has in making a play on it. However, her hit must be flat. It is useless if it bounces. She must keep her eyes on the ball and step toward it as she hits it. This requires a great amount of practice.

11. *Question:* After a wing takes a corner hit, what does she do? Where does she go?

Answer: After the corner hit, the wing goes out as quickly as possible toward the edge of the striking circle so that she will not be offside, she will be in the proper position to help her team, and she will make more space for her inner to work. As she moves out, her opposing halfback moves out with her to mark her.

12. *Question:* Does a wing have to learn how to bully?

Answer: Yes. Whenever the ball goes out over the side line off the sticks of two players, simultaneously, the wings on that side of the field where the ball went out of bounds restart the game with a bully just inside the side line where the ball left the field.

If the ball is hit over the end line by the attack, between the side line and the five-yard line, the wings on that side of the field where the ball went out of bounds restart the game with a bully on the 25-yard line. This 25-yard line bully must be taken opposite the spot on the end line where the ball went out of bounds.

13. *Question:* What part does the wing play in a roll-in when her team is attacking?

Answer: When a team player takes a roll-in, the wing must be ready to cut and leave her opposing halfback behind, she must be in a position to receive the ball, and she must pass it immediately to a team player. To save time, the wing usually takes the roll-in when the play is in the vicinity of her opponent's goal.

Pointers for a Wing:

A GOOD WING:

DOES NOT	BUT ⟶ DOES
1. Lack mobility of body movement.	1. Keep her feet facing in the direction in which she wants to run, turn her head and shoulders, and watch the ball until it is on her stick.
2. Lack excellent stickwork and footwork.	2. Get in a stinging, accurate shot for a goal from a solo run, or a flick from a strategic angle.
3. Lack training or concentration.	3. Judge her time for passing the ball at an opportune moment. To do this, she must look up and analyze the situation.
4. Encroach on the inner's ground because this would confine the inside forwards and inhibit their movements.	4. *Keep out* in the alley to give her opposing defenses a more difficult job, making them cover larger spaces and more ground. By keeping out, she allows passes to come to her in front and not from behind.

DOES NOT	BUT ⟶ DOES
5. Merely run fast. No matter how fast she can run, if she does not dribble closely the opposing halfback will nip in and remove the ball.	5. Run fast with the ball under control.
6. Fail to attempt to use a variety of tactics.	6. Dodge her halfback opponent, using a dodge, a pass to her other forwards, or a solo run, with a hard drive or flick at the goal.
7. Allow the opposing halfback to gain position between herself (the wing) and the ball, because this would make it difficult for her own defense to pass to her.	7. Keep moving, making it difficult for her opposing halfback to mark her and making possible, through her good positioning, a successful clearing hit by her own defense.
8. Make a poor hit to the center or inner when taking a corner hit. A hopped or bumped ball would be too difficult for her forward to stop with accuracy.	8. Make a well-placed, hard, flat hit to the center or inner when taking a corner hit, which may result in a goal being scored.

Inners

Inners must be "goal getters," have commanding control of the ball, be quick to think and act, pass with speed, deception and accuracy, be aggressive, and have stamina.

1. *Question:* Where does the inner go and what does she do at a center bully?

   Answer: She usually stands well away from the bully and runs quickly forward to any pass ahead of her which she hopes to receive.

2. *Question:* If the ball is passed to the inner from the center bully what should she do with it?

   Answer: Get it and control it; then move into the space ahead of her, watch the movements of the opposing fullback, and react according to her opponent's actions.

3. *Question:* What is the inner's job when she has possession of the ball?

   Answer: When on the attack, the inner should dribble, at full speed, the shortest and straightest way to the goal without crowding the center. She should draw her defense (that is, make her opponent act before she

FIG. 115. An inner should
have perfect ball control
and agile footwork.

does), and outwit her by making unexpected dodges
and passes. She must be ready and able to shoot
quickly and hard from the edge of the striking circle,
and to rush the goal.

4. *Question:* In what way can the inner avoid or outwit the opposing fullback who is marking her closely in the
circle?

Answer: A fullback who marks closely in the circle is usually
pulled out if the inner drops out towards the wing,
keeps changing position, or makes sudden runs in toward the goal. The marking fullback is kept off balance by the inner who is moving about.

5. *Question:* Does an inner tackle back?

Answer: Yes. After an inner loses the ball, she tries to retrieve
it immediately.

6. *Question:* Where should the inner go for a roll-in or a free hit
taken by her own defense, and what should she do?

Answer: For a roll-in and free hit taken by her team player,
the inner should pull away from the ball to one side
or the other, forward or backward, to make an opening. She must anticipate a through pass or a flat pass,

and should move as soon as her team player starts her roll or her swing.

On receiving a pass or a roll-in from her defense, she should field the ball and pass it to any one of her forwards. She should make the most opportune pass to outwit her opposing defense, and then rush to get on line with her other forwards.

For a roll-in or free hit made by an opponent, the inner should mark her opposing inner, putting herself in position (between her opponent and the direction from which the ball might come) where she thinks she can intercept the ball that is about to be played by the opponent.

7. *Question:* What part does an inner play on a corner hit?

Answer: On a corner hit, if the inner receives the ball she must: 1) control the ball close to her stick; 2) make a quick, accurate shot for goal; 3) rush her own shot; and, 4) get back toward the edge of the striking circle ready for a defense clear, which may turn into another attack.

On a corner hit, if one of her team players receives the ball, the inner rushes almost all shots for goal. This requires anticipation. She must be able to judge where the ball may go if it bounces from the goalkeeper's pads. If the ball should rebound in her direction, she makes a shot at goal and positions herself for another defense clear, so that she will not be offside.

Pointers for an Inner:

A GOOD INNER:

DOES NOT	BUT ⟶ DOES
1. Lack persistence on the field.	1. Work very hard—one minute tackling back, and the next minute making an assault in the circle, marking at a roll-in, receiving and using a corner hit, or bullying at the 25-yard line.
2. Have difficulty in getting the ball.	2. Have the ability to twist easily and try to keep her feet facing her attacking goal, saving time in turning.

DOES NOT	BUT ⟶ DOES
3. Remain as a standing target making it easy for her opponent to mark her.	3. *Move,* and at varying rates with thought and reason behind her movement.
4. Hang back, wander, or turn her back to the goal which is being attacked.	4. Play in *front* of a halfback, fullback, and center halfback, all of whom would like to give her constructive passes if she is in position and looks ready to receive them.
5. Try always to be in possession of the ball.	5. Distribute the ball to the right and left (always trying to cancel out a defense player), sometimes letting it pass her, sometimes ready to follow up other shots at the goal besides her own.
6. Avoid attempting shots at the goal.	6. Aim for those small spaces near the goalposts which are so difficult for goalkeepers to mark and cover.

Center Forward

Good judgment, excellent stickwork, passing accuracy, and body control are essential for the center forward position.

1. *Question:* What part does the center forward play?

    Answer: The center forward acts as a pivot, guide, and leader for the forward line. She must stay in position in the center of the field, which limits the area in which she has to work. She must have an awareness of the whole game and must distribute the game intelligently, make well-timed, well-placed, sympathetic passes, and make for coordinated play and teamwork on the forward line.

2. *Question:* If the center forward must stay in the center of the field, doesn't this result in close marking by her center halfback?

    Answer: Yes. This means that she must have command of many strokes and be able to perform them with facility in the smallest spaces as she runs; and she must have excellent ball control, controlled stickwork, agile footwork, and quick reaction time in maneuvering in a limited space. She changes her pace and receives passes of any kind from any direction.

She must be able to, 1) think ahead; 2) constantly move and adjust each time the ball is hit in order to pull her opposing center halfback out of position and make a larger opening for a pass; and, 3) cut quickly and dart.

3. *Question:* What is the first thing a center forward should do?

   Answer: Win the bully. To do this she must be able to execute at least three different kinds of bullies and practice them frequently.

4. *Question:* Does the center forward have many scoring possibilities?

   Answer: The center forward has many chances to score goals, and, by her passes, gives her team players opportunities to score. She must be proficient at shooting and have the speed and strength to rush the moment a shot for goal has been made.

5. *Question:* How does a center forward know whether to intercept a hard center pass across the field from her wing or to leave it for her inner?

FIG. 116. Scoring a goal. Perfect for its power, timing, and execution A center forward must take quick advantage of openings for shots.

Answer: This depends upon the position of the center forward when receiving the ball. She must never attempt to stop the ball if she is not certain of success. She will spoil the pass for the inner behind or beside her if she deflects the ball, and thereby waste the whole movement.

6. *Question:* Does the center forward tackle back?

Answer: A center forward must tackle back immediately in order to try to get the ball, or spoil her opponent's play.

7. *Question:* At a corner hit, what is the center forward's objective?

Answer: On a corner hit, she must be ready to receive the ball and control it, and she must be quick to execute a hard, accurate shot for goal.

Pointers for a Center Forward:

A GOOD CENTER FORWARD:

DOES NOT	BUT ⟶ DOES
1. Favor the left side of the field because it is easier to pass in that direction in the early stages.	1. Distribute and vary the play by giving decisive passes using both sides of the field.
2. Wander.	2. Stay in position except when she interchanges with her inner. This is a planned tactic and a purposeful move which necessitates a good understanding with her inside forwards.
3. Continually let her opponent gain possession of the ball after the completion of the bully.	3. Practice taking bullies and know many variations of the bully so that she can, by excellent stickwork and footwork, gain possession of the ball and start the game moving.
4. Remain still, because a stationary player is easy to mark. She does not lack speed or good ball control, or hit the ball without thought.	4. Remain alert to find a small working space and ready to move into it quickly to take a pass or to make a pass that is well-placed, well-timed, and intelligent.
5. React slowly when shooting for a goal.	5. Shoot for a goal quickly when inside the circle. It is the speed at which the hit is made rather than the actual strength of the shot which counts.
6. Stand and watch her own shot at the goal.	6. Shoot quickly and accurately, and *follow up* her shots.

Pointers for a Forward Line Player:

A GOOD FORWARD LINE PLAYER:

DOES NOT	BUT ——————▸ DOES
1. Stop concentrating if she is waiting for the ball or stop working any moment of the game no matter where the play is taking place.	1. Observe her own defense with the ball, note where her own particular opponent is standing, and observe the positions of the other members of her forward line in relation to herself.
2. Fail to shift and adjust each time the ball is hit, in order to be in position to field the ball and advance it forward.	2. Shift and adjust her position each time a player has passed the ball to a space or to another player, in order to be ready for any type of pass from any direction.
3. Stop moving or changing her position every time the ball is hit. She should be facing properly to pick up any kind of a pass from any direction quickly and easily.	3. Watch her own forwards, and face in the right direction with her stick close to the ground, and place herself in the proper position to shoot for a goal.
4. Wait for her defense to obtain the ball for her if she loses it.	4. Tackle back at once if she loses the ball. If she does not regain possession of the ball, at least she forces a hurried and possibly inaccurate pass by her opponent.
5. Go straight for the goal when in possession of the ball.	5. Continue to take the ball with her or pass it according to the position of all other players (her own forward line and her opposing defense) at the moment. If she is free, she goes straight for the goal without hesitation and at the same time looks up and sights the space or forward she will pass to, if necessary.
6. Remain stationary with her opponent marking her.	6. Enlarge the space and get free if her opponent is close by.
7. Remain unaware when her opponent stays in the middle of the space and has left her unmarked.	7. Tackle her opponent if her opponent should intercept an inaccurate pass made by her team player.
8. Stand still if her own defense player has possession of the ball in mid-field and does not seem to be hurried.	8. Anticipate the pass and run as the ball is being hit, to be in the correct position to get the ball or for the next play.
9. Stand and watch after shooting for a goal.	9. Rush after shooting for a goal.

Wing Halfbacks

Wing halfbacks should have speed, anticipation, stamina, reliability, and a sense of awareness.

1. *Question:*   What is the responsibility of the wing halfback?
   Answer: A wing halfback backs up her own forwards when on the attack. She must even get as far as the edge of the circle to shoot goals. She also marks the opposing wing or takes part in the covering tactics of her own defense. This means that she must be able to run as fast as the fastest forward on her own team in order to back up and press the attack, as she must be as fast as the fastest forward on the opposing team in order to defend successfully her own goal. This is a continuous pace throughout the whole game.

2. *Question:*   What are the duties of the wing halfback when her team is attacking?
   Answer: When on the attack she must:
   a. Back up her attacking forwards, and if the ball is

Fig. 117. Reverse or backward roll to the left fullback. Note all the players ready and waiting with their sticks down.

cleared out by the opposing defense, try to intercept it and return it to her forwards.

b. Score goals, whenever she has an opportunity to
do so, with hard, accurate drives or flicks for goal.

c. Be able to cover spaces in order to intercept any
clearing shots made by the defense.

d. Be constantly alert and on the move to shift her
position every time the ball changes direction.

e. Be able to give direct, sympathetic, through passes
to her own forwards while they are moving at top
speed.

f. Be able to roll-in quickly, accurately, forcefully,
and with deception and variety.

g. Have a thorough knowledge of, and be able to use,
the various strokes, tackles, dodges, and passes.

h. Have sustained speed, stamina, and endurance in
order to back up her own forwards when on the
attack.

i. Give hard passes across to the inner or wing on
the opposite side of the field. These diagonal
passes serve two purposes: they divert the opposing defense, and they give an overworked attack
a few valuable moments in which to collect and
sort themselves out.

3. *Question:* What are the duties of the wing halfback when her
team is on the defense?

   Answer: When on the defense she must:

a. Mark: if the ball is on her side of the field, she
must mark her opposing wing. Her responsibility
is to mark the wing on the ball side, to block the
opening for any passes through, and to intercept
the ball, thereby preventing it from reaching the
opponent.

b. Anticipate: move as the ball moves, anticipating
its probable direction; and be ready and alert to
receive or intercept the ball.

c. Cover: be ready to take the place of the fullback
if the situation warrants it and to intercept any
diagonal passes from the opponents.

d. Be a sure tackler: be able to tackle and gain possession of the ball and initiate the attack.

e. Take roll-ins and free hits quickly and vary them decisively and with purpose.

4. *Question:* Where does the halfback go when her team starts the attack?

   Answer: The halfback moves up in back of her inner and wing, keeping out until the wing approaches the circle. When her own forwards are attacking in the circle, the halfback plays a few yards behind the inner and slightly toward the wing, in position to intercept any passes which might come out of the circle from the opposing defense to their inner or wing.

5. *Question:* After the halfback has successfully tackled the opposing wing, what does she do?

   Answer: Following the completion of a tackle, the halfback must consider how and where the opposing defense are situated. She may:
   a. Pass the ball to any one of her own forwards appearing to be in a good position to start an attack.
   b. Give a short pass to her wing, inner, or center forward.
   c. Give a hard pass across the field to her inner or wing, depending upon the opposing defense positions.

6. *Question:* Should a wing halfback ever try to shoot for goal?
   Answer: Yes, whenever the opportunity arises.

7. *Question:* Where does the wing halfback go when her opponents are attacking on the opposite side of the field in her defending half?

   Answer: The wing halfback leaves her opposing wing, temporarily, and moves back and in to mark her opposing inner, permitting her own fullback to move over to cover.

8. *Question:* Is it true that a halfback should never pass the ball across the center of the field?

   Answer: A wing halfback never passes the ball across the center when she is in or near her defending goal, or even in her defending 25-yard area. However, in the attacking 25-yard area, the wing halfback can make a valuable pass to her inner on the opposite side of the field.

9. *Question:* Does a halfback have any special plans for roll-ins?
   Answer: Yes. All roll-ins are made with a purpose in mind and special schemes are arranged with various members of the team.

   a. If the halfback's team is in the opponent's half of the field and she is taking the roll-in, she may use a long roll-in close to the side line for her wing, or a short roll which goes directly to her inner or wing. Sometimes a short reverse roll-in to the fullback is used, if the fullback is ready for it. This roll-in must never be used near one's own defensive end.

   b. If the halfback is taking the roll-in in her own defensive area, it is best to use a long roll-in to the wing, close to the side line, and to keep the ball as far away from her own circle as possible.

Pointers for a Wing Halfback:

A GOOD WING HALFBACK:

DOES NOT	BUT ──────▶ DOES
1. Lack knowledge of the positions of the rest of the team in relation to herself.	1. Have a sense of awareness, so that her passes can be given quickly and accurately.
2. Lack speed of thought for intelligent positioning.	2. Anticipate. She gets into the best position to receive or intercept the pass.
3. Lack speed in changing direction: backwards, forwards, sideways.	3. Recover quickly to be back on defense, and back up her forwards on attack when needed.
4. Overuse one roll-in.	4. Have a variety of roll-ins.
5. Fail to tackle back on the opposing wing who has passed her.	5. Turn around to tackle back on her opponent immediately.

Center Halfback

A center halfback must have stamina, intelligence, agility, and speed.

1. *Question:* What are the duties of the center halfback?
   Answer: The center halfback backs up her own forwards to play attack, and marks closely the center forward of the opposing team when her own team is on the defense.

FIG. 118. Center halfback giving a pass which is being intercepted.

2. *Question:* What are the duties of the center halfback when on the defense?

 Answer: She positions herself between her opposing center forward and the ball, on the goal side. She marks her opposing center forward very closely, to prevent her opponent from getting her stick to the ball. She moves with the opposing center forward and tries to stay as close as a yard from her at all times. The defending center halfback tries to intercept the ball and start an attacking movement.

3. *Question:* Does the center halfback ever score goals? If she goes into the striking circle to shoot, who marks her center forward?

 Answer: Yes, the center halfback should always be ready to try to score a goal whenever the opportunity arises. Sometimes the wings pass back to her near the edge of the striking circle. If she is drawn into the circle when attempting to score, there must be an understanding that her center forward will immediately begin to drop back into her place. However, the center halfback usually will shoot from the edge of the circle, in which case she is ready to turn and get back to mark her opposing center forward in case the attack fails.

4. *Question:* When the center halfback is left behind by her opposing center forward, who takes her place in the defense?

   Answer: If the center halfback loses her center forward, there is only one thing for her to do—turn around and chase her. The center halfback is responsible for the center forward.

5. *Question:* Many times the fullbacks and wing halfbacks change places in defense. Does the center halfback take part in this maneuvering?

   Answer: No. The center halfback is the pivot, the player around whom the other four defense players move.

6. *Question:* What is the main job of the center halfback when her team has been awarded a corner or penalty corner?

   Answer: When her team is given a corner or penalty corner, the center halfback should back up her team players—the center forward, and the inner on the side of the corner hit. She is then in position to send the ball back into the circle if her own forwards miss it, and in position to shoot for goal herself if the occasion arises.

7. *Question:* When the opponents have been awarded a corner or penalty corner, where should the defending center halfback stand, and where should she go when the corner hit is taken?

   Answer: When a corner hit is awarded to the opposing team, the defending center halfback positions herself behind the goal line opposite her opposing center forward. It may mean positioning just outside the goalpost on whichever side the corner hit is being taken, inside the goal cage with the goalkeeper. As soon as the ball is hit, the center halfback must run straight out to the opposing center forward as fast as she can to mark her, or to tackle her, if she receives the ball.

Pointers for a Center Halfback:

A GOOD CENTER HALFBACK:

DOES NOT	BUT ⟶ DOES
1. Wander all over the field.	1. Play in the center of the field.
2. Keep passing the ball to the left all the time.	2. Distribute the play.
3. Hold on to the ball too long, dribbling it up a bit farther, wondering where to pass.	3. Start the attack as soon as possible to prevent the opposing defense from repositioning and covering all the spaces again, or tackling.
4. "Give up" when the game is fast and changes from end to end quickly.	4. Attack and get back to defend, which requires moving all the time.

Fullbacks

Fullbacks must have speed and good footwork, in order to dodge quickly and successfully under all conditions, and perfect ball control, in order to pass in any direction.

1. *Question:* What is meant by fullbacks working together to cover?

   Answer: One fullback must always be in good covering position, well back toward the center of the field. The other fullback, on whose side the ball is in play, stays well up near the halfbacks, backs up her forward line when her team is on the attack, and marks her opponent when her team is on the defense. When the ball is in the center of the field or on the right side, both fullbacks cover deep. As the ball changes from one side of the field to the other, fullbacks alter their positions up and back.

2. *Question:* The fullback marks the opposing inner in the field. What does this mean?

   Answer: The fullback is responsible for the inner. It is her duty to:

   a. Prevent her opponent from getting the ball.

   b. Tackle her, if she does gain possession of the ball,

and take it away from her; and if the circumstances are not right for either (a) or (b); then

    c. Time her movements to force her opponent to pass, so that with proper anticipation one of her team players can get the ball.

3. *Question:* Does the fullback ever cross the center line?

  Answer: When her own team is on the attack, the distance a fullback goes up the field depends entirely on her speed and her ability to turn very quickly and recover. If she is very fast, she can go up to the attacking 25-yard line, but she must be ready to get back quickly. If she lacks speed, she should not go very far beyond the center line.

4. *Question:* Does the fullback ever go out to tackle the wing?

  Answer: The only time the fullback tackles the wing is when the halfback has been left behind. The fullback then delays her tackle until the wing is actually at the edge of the striking circle. The tackle is made to prevent the wing from making a shot at goal or to force

FIG. 119. The fullback did not go out to tackle the wing. The half-back was able to reach the wing before shooting for a goal as she entered the striking circle.

her to pass. The fullback knows that if the latter happens, the fullback, who is playing with her, will have had time and opportunity to position herself to deal with the attacking inner. Through delaying the tackle, the halfback may have had time to resume defense and become the covering player.

5. *Question:* If the ball is on the left side of the defending circle, does the right fullback stay close to her opposing left inner?

    Answer: No. The right fullback leaves her opposing left inner, because she knows that in this instance her right halfback will mark the left inner; the right fullback moves across the circle and back to cover. However, if the ball is passed back quickly to the right side, the right halfback who was marking the left inner must move out to mark her opposing left wing, and the right fullback must get back to mark her left inner as quickly as possible.

6. *Question:* What does the fullback do when the corner hit is taken on the other side?

    Answer: For corners on the other side, the fullback moves to cover, as quickly as possible, with her stick on the ground. She stays near the goal, taking care not to block the goalkeeper's view.

Pointers for a Fullback:

A GOOD FULLBACK:

DOES NOT	BUT ⟶ DOES
1. Retreat into her own striking circle as the opposing inner is coming down the field.	1. Meet her opponent well up the field, if possible.
2. Play with the idea that it does not make any difference -if the ball passes her because the goalkeeper is in back of her.	2. Work with her other fullback as though they were both on a see-saw, covering one another.
3. Rush in to tackle and allow herself to be left out of the defense plan because of poorly timed movement.	3. Wait for the decisive moment before tackling the opponent.
4. Concentrate on ineffective, long drives which can be fielded by the opposite defense.	4. Concentrate on accurate, sympathetic passes to her team player.

Pointers for a Defense Player:

A GOOD DEFENSE PLAYER:

DOES NOT	BUT ⟶ DOES
1. Work only when her team is on the defense.	1. Work together with her other halfbacks and fullbacks and play as a unit whether her team is on the attack or defense.
2. Fail to realize that she plays a very important part in the attack by backing up her forwards in a position to cover all openings in order to intercept clearing shots and get the ball back to her own forwards for a further attack.	2. Back up her forward line closely; watch every move intently, anticipating the probable direction of the clearing shot and placing herself in relation to the position of the ball; and keep her opponent well marked.
3. Hang back when her team is on the defense.	3. Tackle her opposing forward or the backfield player who has the ball.
4. Give up when outwitted by her opponent.	4. Tackle back at once to regain possession of the ball from the opposing player who took it away.
5. Fail to place herself between the goal and the ball-side of her opponent when opposing forwards have the ball.	5. Anticipate the play and shift into a position to tackle or intercept the ball and place her team immediately on the attack.

Goalkeeper

The goalkeeper position requires courage, alertness, good judgment, and reliability.

1. *Question:* What should a goalkeeper wear to keep warm and yet be free for action?

   Answer: It is very important for a goalkeeper to keep warm, but clothing must be comfortable and light and must not restrict her movements. Warm, winter underwear, slacks, warm-up pants or ski pants, a light windbreaker, a long wool sweater, and gloves are essential.

2. *Question:* How should the goalkeeper hold her stick?

   Answer: The goalkeeper should hold her stick in her right hand, rather than in both, to increase her reach side-

ways and aid body balance. It also leaves her left
hand free for raised balls.

3. *Question:* What is the duty of the goalkeeper?
   Answer: The goalkeeper has the final responsibility of keeping the ball out of the goal.

FIG. 120. A satisfying moment. Having anticipated
the shot, this goalkeeper
was able to give a good
clearance to her forwards
to start an attacking
movement.

4. *Question:* What does the goalkeeper use to stop the ball?
   Answer: The goalkeeper may stop the ball with her hand or
   stick, but she stops it primarily with her legs and
   feet or instep.

   a. If the ball comes at her in the air, she stops the
   ball with her hand, drops it on the ground, and
   makes a clear. However, if she bats or throws
   away the raised ball with her hand, she is penal-
   ized.

   b. If the attack hits a well-directed shot to the goalkeeper's right when the goalkeeper is covering or
   blocking the left of the goal, the goalkeeper
   lunges to the right and reaches over with her
   stick to save the ball.

   c. It is not advisable to hit the ball on the fly with
   the stick because it may be lifted off the ground
   into an attacking player, which is dangerous and
   a foul.

d. If the attack shoots and the forward line rushes the shot at goal or bears down on her, the goalkeeper may kick the ball or clear it with her stick. This is an individual choice. She uses her stick when her anticipation is not quick enough to get her feet to the ball.

5. *Question:* Where does the goalkeeper take her position?

Answer: The goalkeeper takes her position about a yard in front of the goal line.

Some goalkeepers make marks on the ground in front of each goalpost; others make a cross in the center, a known distance forward; and still others may do both. However, the player's awareness of the exact position of the goal behind her comes with experience. The striking circle will help to some extent, provided it is clearly marked.

6. *Question:* How should a goalkeeper stand to stop and clear the ball with her feet?

Answer: The goalkeeper places herself directly behind the oncoming ball, with her feet together, knees slightly bent, weight evenly balanced, and body crouched forward. As the ball hits the pads, she bends her knees forward, which traps the ball and tends to make it drop in front of her, close to her feet. She then does a swinging clear, using the inside of her foot (along the big toe and instep), the outside of her foot (just above the little toe joint), the instep, or the toe end of her boot.

If she is on the left side of the goal, she clears the ball to the left with her right foot by swinging her foot to the side, keeping her weight low and finishing with her weight on the right foot or clearing foot. On the right side of the goal she uses her left foot.

7. *Question:* How can a goalkeeper be ready for any type of shot from any angle?

Answer: As the ball approaches and enters the striking circle, she aligns herself with the ball according to the way the play develops. On every shot, she places herself squarely between the ball and the goal—to her left,

if the ball is coming on her left and to the right if
the attack is developing on her right.

8. *Question:* Where should the goalkeeper clear the ball?

    Answer: A goalkeeper must be able to make a perfect, low,
    accurate clear to any desired spot, preferably side-
    ways and parallel to the goal line. However, there
    are times when she may pass the ball directly on to
    the stick of a team player or into a space.

9. *Question:* Does a goalkeeper ever leave her position to go out
    to tackle?

    Answer: The goalkeeper should go out:

    a. If she thinks she can get the ball while it is out
    of control of the forward.

    b. If she thinks she can spoil the forward's shot at
    goal.

    c. If there is a ball in no one's possession coming
    toward the striking circle and she thinks she can
    get it.

10. *Question:* How far forward should a goalkeeper go?

    Answer: a. The distance a goalkeeper moves out in front of
    her cage varies with the situation.

    b. Much more of the goal is covered when the goal-
    keeper uses the forward space than if she stays
    on the goal line.

    c. The farther forward the goalkeeper advances, the
    more of the goal she covers insofar as the player
    in front of her is concerned, but the more she un-
    covers for those at the side. When the ball is com-
    ing from the inner, or wing position, the angle
    is narrowed so that she does not have to go so
    far forward to cover the goal.

    d. A goalkeeper may move forward to get a rising
    ball (scoop) before it reaches its greatest pos-
    sible height; however, if she leaves too much
    space behind her, she may be beaten, because
    she will find that her forward position coincides
    with the highest point of the scoop. A scoop of
    this height is generally advertised sufficiently
    ahead of time for an alert goalkeeper to move
    back the necessary distance.

FIG. 121. Goalkeeper on ball side of cage, crouched and in a ready position.

FIG. 122. One of the most thrilling experiences for a goalkeeper occurs when she has left her goal at the right moment to meet an oncoming forward. This is one of the most difficult things to do, as timing is very important.

Pointers for a Goalkeeper:

A GOOD GOALKEEPER:

DOES NOT	BUT ⟶ DOES
1. Let the ball rebound away from her.	1. Keep rebounds very close to her pads by bending her knees.
2. Fail to concentrate.	2. Constantly reposition herself for whatever attack may develop.
3. Work without understanding or sympathy for the other defense players.	3. Act as a steadying influence on her defense, particularly when they are hard pressed. She gives steady, calm words of encouragement. She directs defense play, when necessary, to keep her teammates from blocking her view of the ball.
4. Take her eyes off the ball.	4. Anticipate the angle of the shot and place herself directly on line with it.

Fig. 123. Practicing techniques or strokes may be done individually, in pairs with a partner or an opponent, and in groups.

154

6

For players at all levels, the key to improvement of field hockey performance is well-directed practice. Stickwork games can be extremely valuable, both in the practice of the actual strokes and for improving the stickwork involved in certain tactics and combinations. However, it is important that the exact point aimed at in the practice of the moment should be absolutely clear in the minds of the coach and the players.

Worthwhile activities should be made significant to the student. She may not realize that a certain activity needs more drill; there must, therefore, be a skillful pattern of varied methods of presentation and of formations for practice. The relation and application of each activity to the whole game should be shown to keep up interest. Points of *good* form, as well as errors, should be analyzed on the basis of the mechanics of movement involved. The most significant errors, common

Practice for Progress

to a large number of the group, should be pointed out first: then, individual errors.

Each instructor must use her own discretion as to the method of procedure and progression she will use, because every situation and each group of players present a different problem. Motivation to improve can be high, and practice can be pleasurable and competitive, *if the coach so guides it.* The desire for improvement of individual and team performance will gradually come from the players themselves.

Practicing techniques or strokes may be done individually, in pairs (with a partner or an opponent), and in groups. The instructor must make certain that practice periods are a learning situation and at the same time fun—not boring or tiresome. As a step in progression, the practice of strokes and techniques should be presented in game form, some involving no competition and others using competition, because whatever is being stressed can be carried over directly into the actual game situation and will be more satisfying and enjoyable for the players. For training and drills for field hockey, only a ball, a stick, and a small area are needed to make a start.

This chapter deals with drills and games for practicing various combinations and tactics. However, these should be considered merely as *suggested* activities to be used as a guide in helping to improve the game of hockey.

There is no doubt that athletic training and exercise are extremely valuable for the general fitness and muscular coordination of hockey players. General stamina usually improves with general fitness. To build up stamina for any kind of sport, one should do a great deal of running and sprinting and should take part regularly in the particular activity for which skill and endurance is to be built. For example, good hockey players would not be good unless they played hockey often. It is always best to obtain specialized coaching, if at all possible, in order to learn fundamental skills correctly and prevent the development of bad habits. Moreover, coaches, as teachers, have inspirational responsibilities.

A great help toward achievement of real speed in play can be the practice of ten-yard bursts from a standing position, using small steps for the initial thrust. Improving anticipation can stimulate speed off the mark also. Other good drills are fast and slow running, relay racing, jogging, 60-yard dashes, sprint starts, and changing direction rapidly. Many hockey players would benefit from general warming up with some exercises before matches. They should be repeated several times, with gradual increase in length for development of real endurance.

It is within the ability of any player to increase her speed, but she must realize that much time and hard work are involved. However, once a certain peak has been reached, it is possible to retain this speed with a minimum of training.

One important way to strengthen the left hand and wrist is to carry the hockey stick in the left hand, when jogging, with the head of the stick toward the ground. Another method is to squeeze a tennis ball in the left hand repeatedly. Left-hand strength may also be increased by dribbling once around the field, using the left hand only. An excellent indoor practice that is good for footwork is to roll a ball in a sock, place it on the floor, and play with it with the hockey stick, turning the stick in every possible way to improve skill in handling the stick. These simple routines are suggested to show that valuable practice may be had even when a player is alone, in a house, and with little or no equipment.

Drills

(1) Place several lines of players one behind the other in back of a starting line.

The first player in each line dribbles the ball, in as straight a line as possible, up to a designated person, object, or line, turns or goes around the obstacle, clockwise, dribbles the ball back to the stick of the next girl in line, and goes to the end of the line. The second player repeats, and the play continues until each one has had an opportunity to dribble.

Note: Dribbling, page 23; Stick ready to take ball—position of readiness, page 19.

Variations:

a. Dribble up, turn clockwise, and either stop the ball and pass it or pass the ball, while running, to the next player in line, using a variety of strokes. As soon as the ball has been hit, the next player in line starts forward to receive it. The player who has passed the ball goes to the end of the line.

Note: Receiving the ball, page 66; Stopping the ball, page 33; Strokes which may be used: (a) Push, page 38, (b) Drive, page 26, (c) Flick, page 45.

b. Increase the distance as players become more skilled with increased speed, and then use as relays.

(2) Line up any number of players in columns about ten yards apart. Have an even number of columns so that players may work in pairs.

Players working in couples use one ball for each couple. Player on the right sends a short, easy drive diagonally forward to the player on the left, who runs forward to receive the pass and immediately returns the ball, using a short diagonal push pass forward to the player on the right. Continue to a designated spot, change direction, repeat performance back to place, give or pass the ball to the next couple in line, and go to the end of own column.

Note: Carrying position of the stick, page 20; Passing, page 59; Receiving the ball, page 66; Push pass, page 38; Drive, page 26.

Variations:

a. Both players use a diagonal drive forward.

Note: Drives—left, page 31; right, page 29; wrist, page 32.

b. Player on the left dribbles and the player on the right uses the left-hand lunge tackle. Repeat several times. Turn around and repeat the same procedure until back to place.

Note: Left-hand lunge, page 41.

c. Player on the right dribbles and the player on the left uses a circular tackle. Continue for a designated number of times to execute the tackle; turn around, and repeat on way back to own line, with the player now on the right dribbling and the player on the left using a circular tackle.

Note: Circular tackle, page 49.

d. Same as "c," except that the player on the right dribbles, and the player on the left attempts a reverse stick tackle.

Note: Reverse stick tackle, page 53.

e. Same as "d," except that player on the left attempts a right jab.

Note: Right jab, page 55.

f. Same as "b," except that the player on the right uses a left jab.

Note: Left jab, page 55.

(3) Same formation as Number 2. Place an obstacle or player directly in front of each line about 10 feet away from the first player in each column. The first player dribbling the ball must scoop it over the obstacle or the player's stick, reverse her direction with a turn, dribble and scoop over the obstacle or stick again, dribble the ball back to the next player in line, and go to the end of the column.

Note: Scoop, page 50.

Variations:

a. Dodges
   1) Push to the right, page 47.
   2) Pull to the left, page 39.
   3) Pull to the right with reverse stick, page 52.
b. Strokes: Use jab stroke—left and right; page 55.

(4) Use an even number of columns, 2, 4, 6, 8, and so forth. Column 1 faces column 2, with about 25 yards between the first two players in each column. Column 3 faces column 4. The first player in each of the odd-numbered columns, 1, 3, 5, 7, and so on, should start with a ball.

Player with the ball dribbles forward; player without the ball, standing opposite, moves forward to tackle the player dribbling. Player who gains possession of the ball will continue in the same line of direction as she started, give the ball to the next player in the opposite column, and go to the end of that column. The player who lost possession of the ball will continue to move forward to the end of the opposite column from where she started.

Note: Straight tackle, page 36.

Variations:

a. Tackles
   1) Left-hand lunge, page 41.
   2) Reverse stick tackle, page 53.
b. Dodges
   1) Push to the right, page 47.
   2) Pull to the left, page 39.
   3) Scoop, page 50.

(5) Line up players in three columns about 10 yards apart, behind the 25-yard line and facing the striking circle.

The first player in each column dribbles to the edge of the striking circle, drives at the goal, recovers her own ball, passes it back to the next player in her column, and goes to the end of her line.

Note: Shooting, page 63; Passing, page 59; Receiving, page 66.

Variations:

a. Increase number of columns to 4, then 5; use one ball. Place the 5 columns in position of a forward line. Increase distance to center line, and use the 25-yard line farthest away from the goal they are facing.

b. Add players to act as opposing defense—first 1 or 2 then 3, 4, 5, and finally 6. Have opposing defense stationary at first, but attempting to tackle, then moving.

> *Note:* Passing, page 59; Receiving, page 66; Intercepting, page 69; Tackling back, page 68; Covering, page 76; Marking, page 73.

c. Add six players to back up the forward line.

> *Note:* Backing up, page 71.

(6) Line up players using both sides and both ends of the field, if necessary. Place one column of players, Line A, along the outside of the side line at one end of the field, and the other column, Line B, diagonally ahead inside the 5-yard line on the field of play, facing in the same direction. Each player in Line A has a ball.

The first player in Line A rolls the ball down the alley, and then moves over to stand at the end of the Line B column. The first player in Line B runs forward, fields the ball, dribbles, turns to her right, and goes back to the end of the opposite column, Line A. The next player in Line A rolls the ball for the next player in Line B to obtain. This procedure continues until all players have had a turn to roll in the ball as well as field the ball.

Note: Roll-In, page 97.

Variations:

a. Both columns of players turn and face in the opposite direction.
b. Vary roll-ins, page 104.

(7) Practice for the goalkeeper—indoors or outdoors. Introduce goalkeeper with softballs and no kicking pads; make certain that she holds her stick but does not use it.

Variations:

a. A player, A, rolls or hits the ball for the goalkeeper, B, to kick to a third player, C. Players A and C can vary their positions hitting and receiving the ball.

> *Note:* After the first trial, discuss the matter of kicking. A goalkeeper is the last line of defense; she *must not* let the ball pass her. The inner side of the foot, being broader than toe, should be used as a tool of preventive play. The goalkeeper must avoid jumping at the ball, but agility should be encouraged from the very start. A "follow-through" with the leg, similar to that used with the stick in hitting,

is an excellent practice drill. The head should be held down to prevent the ball from rising. The goalkeeper should imagine, in drills, that the third person is a member of her own team, and she should kick the ball accurately to her, learning to use either foot with equal skill.

b. Goalkeeper may practice kicking a softball or tennis ball against a wall to develop skill and agility.

c. At the beginning of the session, the goalie may well use a soccer ball. While jogging, dribble, using both feet, keeping the ball under control. Two goalies may stop and kick the ball to each other. In the gymnasium, substitute a tennis ball, which will necessitate extremely fast action for stopping and clearing. Work should be begun without pads, then done with pads. This will develop agility, and eye and foot coordination.

(8) Instruction for marking and covering.

The following drills for marking and covering can be introduced in the gymnasium on a wet day:

Without the ball (forwards stationary): Let five forwards play in one half of the field, and a complete defense in the other half. Show each defense player the opponent for whom she is responsible, and emphasize that she must mark *only* her own opponent. After several games, and when every defense player is sure of the person she is marking normally, explain the covering system. Show each defender where to move, according to the position of the ball. Point to the direction of the imaginary ball. Each defense player runs to her position accordingly.

SUGGESTED MOTIVATION CHART						
Names	Dribble	Stop and Hit	Straight Drive	Push	Left-Hand Lunge	etc.
Adams, Jane						
Bennett, Mary						
Bowdoin, Evelyn						
Brown, Ann						
Carey, Joan						
Case, Mary						
Holmes, June						
Jenkins, Catherine						
Knight, Helen						
Murphy, Helen						
Powers, Eleanor						
Wren, Esther						

With the ball: As soon as the covering is understood, throw the ball, and have the forwards move and the defense mark and cover correctly. Repeat this *many* times, and throw the ball in all possible directions. If the defense can succeed in clearing the ball between two markers placed on the center line on each side, award a score of half a goal each time. Let the forwards score in the usual way.

The motivation chart should be adapted to individual requirements. Names of players are arranged alphabetically and illustrative techniques are listed. Space is made to check off each student (v, +, *, —, O, or other symbols).

Variations of charts for checking techniques can easily be worked out by teachers and coaches to suit their particular needs. Various symbols in black and white, or in colors, handwritten or pasted on the chart, may be used to indicate degrees of skill. Students will watch these progress charts and will compete with themselves and others to complete increasingly higher skills.

INDEX

A

Accidents or interference with game, 17
All-England Women's Hockey Association, 2, 3
Alley, 12, 129
American Association for Health, Physical Education and Recreation of the National Education Association, 5
Applebee, Constance M. K., 1, 2, 3 (fig.), 5
Association teams, player qualifications, 3
Associations, local, 3
Attack players:
  bully, 25-yard line (fig.), 94
  corner (fig.), 111-12
  penalty (figs.), 113-15
  free hit
    center halfback (figs.), 120-23
    right fullback (figs.), 123-26
    right halfback (figs.), 118-20
    right wing (fig.), 117
  roll-in
    right halfback (figs.), 101-03
    right wing (figs.), 104-09
Attacking half, 13

B

Backfield players, in lineup for center bully (fig.), 93
Backing up (figs.), 71-73
Balls, "official" hockey, 8
Boot, goalie, 10, 11
Boston Association, 2
Boston Normal School of Gymnastics, 2
Boundary lines, 12
British College of Physical Education, 1
Bryn Mawr College, first field hockey instruction, 2

Bully:

center (fig.), 86, 93
defense player, backing up, 71
game restarting, 86-87
on attacking team's own 25-yard line, 91
on opponent's 25-yard line, 91
on-the-spot, after temporary suspension of game, 88
penalty (figs.), 88-90, 95-96
striking of sticks (fig.), 89-90
variations, 92-93
wing, 87-88

C

Cane handle of stick, 7
Canvas hockey shoes, 8
Care of field hockey stick, 7, 8
Center, flat passes, 60
Center bully, 14 (fig.), 86
  player lineup, 93
Center forward, participation in:
  bully
    center, 93
    twenty-five yard line (fig.), 94
  corner (fig.), 111-12
  penalty (figs.), 113-15
  free hit
    center halfback, between own 25-yard line and center line (figs.), 120-22
    center halfback, near edge of opponent's striking circle (fig.), 122-23
    right fullback, near goal line outside striking circle (fig.), 123-24
    right fullback, just outside striking circle (fig.), 124-25
    right halfback, between two 25-yard lines in opponent's half of field (fig.), 119-20

Index

165